RECEIVING
ANSWERS TO
OUR PRAYERS

RECEIVING ANSWERS TO OUR PRAYERS

GENE R. COOK

Deseret Book Company
Salt Lake City, Utah

ISBN 0-87579-803-9

Printed in the United States of America

10   9   8   7   6   5   4   3   2   1

To all who desire to give thanks to the Lord
for the many prayers he has answered,
and to all who are struggling
to learn better how to pray.

CONTENTS

Acknowledgments

How thankful I am to the Lord for the blessing he has given of continually answering my prayers over the years. I am grateful to my family and to many other wonderful Latter-day Saints who have shared with me their experiences in receiving answers to prayer. A special thanks is given to those who have shared their struggles in receiving such answers. Without any question, the Lord does answer all humble and sincere prayers, whether we recognize it at the time or not.

Sincere appreciation is expressed to Brother Jay A. Parry, whose excellent editing skills have caused this material to be presented in a more succinct way, thus making it more easily understood. I also appreciate the help of my secretary, Stephanie Colquitt, and former secretaries who typed experiences in my life at the time they occurred so they could be accurately shared with others.

Lastly, I would like to say that this book is not in any way an official publication of The Church of Jesus Christ of Latter-day Saints. Any shortcomings, omissions, or deficiencies are clearly mine as the one solely responsible for the material in this book.

INTRODUCTION

We all need so much from the Lord! We need help in every area of our lives:
- personal failings and weaknesses
- family problems and decisions
- work and career
- important decisions with money
- difficult Church assignments
- dealing with the many trials that come our way
- learning the truth about the gospel
- and just about every other aspect of life.

One vital key to success in all of these things is prayer. When we begin to learn how to obtain answers to our prayers, we are able to tap into the Lord's power and goodness to help us in our lives. But if our prayers are ineffective, or if we don't really learn to rely on the Lord, we're usually left to our own devices.

Often people will say, "I try to pray, but the Lord just doesn't speak to me. I know he lives, and I know he loves me, but he just doesn't answer my prayers. Maybe he wants me to live my life on my own, without his help."

It's true that the Lord wants us to constantly exercise our agency to do good, to grow, to develop, to learn to act for ourselves and not to be acted upon. However, he has promised every one of us the gift to be able to receive constant direction from the Holy Ghost. He has promised to help us in every aspect of our lives, if only we will let him.

I firmly believe that the problem is *never* with the Lord when we don't receive answers to our prayers. He is constant and true; he never fails in any of his promises. Rather, the failing is in us.

Often we just don't know how to obtain the answers we seek. Maybe we're not diligent enough in the seeking, or maybe we ask without listening to the Lord's reply. Maybe we haven't prepared our hearts to receive whatever the Lord might send. Maybe we haven't understood and practiced some of the basic principles he has taught us regarding prayer. Maybe we have allowed our will to dominate and have not truly sought his holy will.

I think the Lord at times must be saddened that while he has offered us so much, we're satisfied with so little. But when we begin to learn how to obtain answers to our prayers, we start to see the divine ways in which the Lord works, and we see we *can* receive the Father's many gifts.

In the pages of this book we will examine some of the very basic principles and practices of prayer, which the Lord has taught us through scripture and through living prophets. We will do our best to illustrate those principles through numerous examples and true-life stories, showing that the Lord does answer prayer and showing how it can work. We will discuss in some depth how you can know when you have received an answer to prayer. We will especially treat the difficult question of why at times it appears you have not received an answer, and what you can do even in those circumstances to increase your faith.

Now, how can you receive the most from this book? I

hope that the ideas we discuss throughout these pages are truly of value to all those who read them. To help you and your family, I have placed some key questions for review at the conclusion of each chapter. I suggest you discuss these questions with someone else, where possible, to further your understanding. The Lord may further teach you both.

The highest level of learning I know of comes directly from the Spirit of the Lord. We can learn much by observing someone else or by reading concepts or doctrines that are taught. But the learning that is of the greatest value to me is that which comes by the Spirit, enlightening the mind and speaking to the heart. Such teachings are really nothing less than a message from the heavens to each of us, and they can have a profound effect on our lives.

I bear my testimony that this kind of learning is available to all those who seek, if they will humble themselves before the Lord and earnestly try to receive his instruction. If you will pray in your heart, with real intent, each time you pick up this book to read, the Lord will inspire you that you may be able to receive the blessings he desires to give you. He will send promptings and impressions to you, and you will know how prayer can bless you—and how you can receive divine direction to help you in every aspect of your life.

CHAPTER 1

THE POWER OF PRAYER

A few years ago our family was invited to vacation at a ranch in Wyoming. One of my sons had just come back from a mission to South America, and we were eager to get away from home so we could spend some time with him and the rest of our children.

We had a wonderful time, even though we were able to ride the horses only during the cool of the day. As the day heated up, the horseflies began to attack, biting the horses so viciously that the blood would literally flow down the horses' sides. Then the horses would get excited and would try to buck us off.

The night before we were to leave, as we were heading back to the ranch house, this son asked if he could keep riding with one of the rancher's sons. "We're going to round up some horses," he said, "and then I'll come in and join the family."

About an hour later he came in very upset. "What's the matter, Son?" I asked.

"I'm really mad," he said. "I lost my hat out there in the fields, and I know we'll never be able to find it."

I knew which hat he was talking about. It was a hat he'd purchased in South America as a remembrance of his mission, and it was irreplaceable to him.

He fretted and complained for a time about his lost

hat, and then he brightened a bit and said, "Dad, what would you think if we got the family together before we left for home in the morning, had a family prayer, and then went out to try to find it?"

"That's a great idea," I said. "We'll get up an hour earlier than we'd planned and see what we can do."

Early the next morning I was out packing the car when he came striding across the courtyard from the bunkhouse where he'd been sleeping. I could tell by his expression that he was even more upset than he'd been the night before.

"Dad, I've had it," he said. "I not only lost my hat, but now my wallet's missing too. They both must be out there in the fields." Then he went into great detail about what his wallet contained—his temple recommend (he'd just had his interviews), his driver's license (just obtained), eighty dollars, which was all the money he had in the world (he'd spent all his money on his mission; the eighty dollars was a gift from his grandparents to help him get started again).

"This is the worst vacation I've ever been on," he said. "I wish I'd never come." And then he added a famous statement we've all heard before: "Why do things like this always happen to me?"

"Well, Son, I don't know about your hat or your wallet," I said, "but I do know one thing for sure—I'm not getting the family together to pray about them."

"Why not?"

"Because you can't hear the voice of the Spirit when you're mad. It won't work, and I'm not going to bring the family together while you have that attitude."

He didn't answer, just turned and stomped off toward the house.

Fifteen or twenty minutes later he came back out. His

countenance had changed, and he said, "Dad, I want to apologize. I shouldn't have said those things. This has been a good vacation, and I'm sorry I complained so much about it."

As we talked I learned he'd been on his knees, confessing his bad attitude to the Lord, asking for forgiveness, and asking for help in finding his hat and wallet. Then he came back to me with a broken heart and a humble spirit.

I put my arm around his shoulder and said, "Son, let's call the family together now. Maybe if we all exercise our faith together we can find your lost items."

We all gathered, knelt, and prayed. We knew we were asking the impossible. We had ridden over hundreds of acres of ground the day before, and most of it was covered with high Wyoming wheat so tall it brushed the horses' bellies as we rode by. Still, we wanted to make the attempt, and we prayed as fervently as we could that the Lord would help us.

My son knew we might not succeed. But he had decided he would accept the Lord's will, that he would be satisfied with the outcome of our search, no matter what it was. He said, "I could always get a new hat, even though I'd feel bad. I could replace the temple recommend and the driver's license. And I could replace the money my grandparents have given me. But I truly hope the Lord will answer our prayer."

After the family prayer, we got on the horses and rode out toward the fields we'd been riding in the day before. When we reached the first field, we got off the horses, stood in a circle, and offered prayer again, asking the Lord to guide us to the spot we needed to find. I had two or three of us take turns praying, knowing that would help to strengthen our faith. We told the Lord that ultimately it didn't matter too much whether or not we succeeded—it was just a hat and a wallet. But we also believed the words that said, "Whatsoever ye shall ask the Father in my name, which is right, believing that ye shall receive, behold it shall be given unto you." (3 Nephi 18:20.)

I was on the lead horse as we entered that first field to begin our search. The wheat was brushing against my horse's belly, and almost without thinking I blurted out, "You could never see a wallet in this deep, tall, dark grass. How could you ever see a wallet in something like this?"

There was dead silence in the family for a moment, and then another son said, "You know, Dad, I guess it doesn't matter how deep the grass is, does it? The Lord knows where the wallet is." Then he added, "Actually, you could double or triple it, if you wanted. It really wouldn't matter, because He knows, doesn't He?"

I knew he was right, and his gentle reminder helped to chasten me for an unbelieving attitude. I said, "You know, children, he is exactly right. Double it, triple it—it doesn't matter. The Lord knows where it is. Just ride and pray. Ride and pray and let's go."

We took off across the fields then, half a dozen of us riding over an area that was as wide as you could see. Not more than a minute or two passed before this son who had just expressed his faith shouted, jumped off his horse, and called out, "I've got the hat!" He grabbed it up and waved it in the air for all of us to see.

We all rushed over to where he was, with the owner of the hat leading the way. "The Lord answered our prayers!" he said. "He heard us and answered us!" Then he gave a little talk to the family about continuing to pray and having more faith. "Now let's find that wallet!"

We took off riding again, but we couldn't find a thing. The time began to drag on and on, and the initial excitement we'd felt at finding the hat began to wane. We searched for an hour, then an hour and a quarter, and could find nothing at all.

Then, as the day began to warm up, the flies began to bite at the horses and at us. In fear and irritation, the horses began to kick and buck, and we all began to be afraid of being thrown into the grass. My younger daughters particularly began to get nervous. Finally I said, "Well, we've got to go back, children. We can't search anymore."

We got on the road and started back to the ranch house. As we rode back I decided, as the father of the family, to sidle up alongside the son who'd lost the hat and wallet to take his temperature spiritually, to see where he was at this key moment.

"Well, Son, how are you feeling about all this?" I asked.

He said, "I'm just so thankful the Lord gave me my hat back. I know it's just a hat to anybody else, but it means a lot to me." He paused, then said, "I wish we'd found the wallet, too. Maybe when they harvest the field they'll find it and send it to me. But I want you to know, Dad, that it was really worth it and I'm thankful I've got my hat."

We rode on in to the ranch house, and I gave thanks to the Lord that his heart was right, that his sail was set correctly. Even though we hadn't found the wallet, he knew the Lord loved him and cared about him—and he continued to have faith that it might still be found.

We arrived back at the ranch house and separated to make our final preparations to go. Most of the children were in the car, and I was saying goodbye to our hosts.

All of a sudden this son came running across the courtyard, waving his hand in the air and yelling, "I've got my
wallet! I've got my wallet!"

After all the excitement, we asked him how he'd
found it. He said, "I went into the bunkhouse to get my
suitcase and, while I was alone, I just felt I ought to kneel
and tell the Lord thanks for helping me to find my hat.

"When I got up off my knees to leave, I had a feeling
I should go over by those old, dirty coats that were hang-
ing against one wall." There was a long row of these
coats, maybe ten to fifteen of them. As he stood there, not
knowing why, suddenly he heard something fall to the
floor at his feet. He looked down and saw his comb.

"When I saw that, my heart just leaped. I never split
up my comb and my wallet, and I realized that I had lost
my comb with my wallet. I reached over and shook the
coats and my wallet fell out onto the floor."

We have no idea how that wallet got into those coats.
None of my children ever played near them—the coats
were too dusty and dirty. But somehow, because of faith
and prayer, the Lord made it possible for my son to find
the wallet he'd lost.

He was overjoyed. He knelt and offered another
prayer of thanks in the bunkhouse, and then came running out with the wallet to tell everyone that our prayers
had been answered and that our faith in the Lord had
been fulfilled.

We got in the car then and drove away, but as soon as
we were off the rancher's property we pulled the car
over again and offered a prayer of pure gratitude, thanking the Lord for his willingness to hear us and bless us.

But perhaps the most important "effects" of this experience were yet to come. As great as it was to find our
son's wallet, a greater blessing was the additional faith

our family members gained as a result of the experience. They also grew in their knowledge of how to obtain answers to prayer. Surely the members of our family could never deny the fact that they saw, in a rather miraculous way, the hand of the Lord revealed on our behalf.

THE SECOND LOST WALLET

A week after we arrived home, a younger son, who was sixteen, was invited to go with a friend's family on their yearly trip to Lake Powell. They had just bought a new boat and were anxious to try it out.

After three or four days of boating, they left their camping spot and went back to the marina. My son brought his wallet, but he didn't have any pockets, so he asked his friend to put the wallet in his shirt pocket and button it. The wallet contained about twenty-five dollars, all his personal cards—driver's license, library card, gym card, and school cards—and, most importantly, a little dental retainer piece that was worth more than seventy-five dollars.

Later in the day they went back to camp and went swimming. They dove off many cliffs and jumped off scores of ledges. All of a sudden my son's friend remembered the wallet in his pocket—and he realized it was gone.

By that time they had been all over that part of the lake. It seemed simply impossible that they would ever find it. But my son said to himself, "If the Lord knew where my brother's wallet was on a big ranch, he knows where mine is in this lake." And he began to pray in his heart. After a few minutes he decided that wasn't enough—and he went behind some tall rocks and knelt down in prayer, asking the Lord to help him find the lost wallet.

They continued to look, diving time after time down to the murky mud at the bottom of that lagoon. They searched through the afternoon and evening but found nothing. Finally it was too dark to continue, and they returned to camp.

That night he offered a prayer. He promised the Lord that if he would help him find his wallet, he would read the scriptures more faithfully, control his thoughts better, not listen to inappropriate music, pray more often, and have better prayers. Then, very importantly, he pledged to honor those promises even if he didn't recover the wallet.

After his prayer he had a very positive feeling from the Spirit. When people asked him if he had found the wallet, he just said, "No, not yet."

That same night he and his friend talked. The friend said he feared it would be impossible to find the wallet. The water was just too deep, and the wallet would have sunk into the dirt and moss at the bottom of the lagoon. My son agreed that the water was deep. But he said that finding the wallet had nothing to do with how deep the water was or how much dirt was on top of it or anything else. He said all that mattered was if they had enough faith and if the Lord wanted them to find it.

After breakfast he and his friend went out looking again. The others in the camp were very discouraging, saying that the wallet would surely never be found and that he ought to just give up.

Finally my son hiked up a hill, found a solitary place, and knelt down and offered another prayer. He told the Lord again that he would keep the promises he'd made whether he found the wallet or not. After the prayer he felt reassured that everything would be all right. He prayed constantly as they continued to dive, looking, but they had no success. They were almost ready to give up when my son's friend yelled, "I found it!"

My son was thrilled—and he was glad his friend was the one who found the wallet, since he still blamed himself for losing it. After thanking his friend, he hiked up the hill again and thanked the Lord with all his heart for showing them where to look. And again he pledged to keep the promises he'd made.

Later, he recorded his testimony of his experience. He testified that

> the Lord helps us in our lives and answers our prayers if we—
>
> 1. Pray and ask sincerely.
> 2. Repent. The faster you heed the Lord, the faster he will heed you.
> 3. Read the scriptures and obtain the Spirit.
> 4. Make promises to do better in areas in which you have problems.
> 5. Get rid of all doubt and anger in your heart.
>
> I testify to you that if you do these things and it is right for you, the Lord will answer your prayer. I know that it was not by luck or chance that we found the wallet, and I know the Lord really did guide me to find it when I was ready. I testify to you that this is true and it really did happen. . . . I have a testimony that the Lord lives and loves each one of us and will help us if we will only reach out to him and obey his commandments.

It was rewarding to see the whole family unite to try to find the hat and wallet of our first son. But it was particularly satisfying to see our younger son exercise sufficient faith to have that kind of experience on his own.

That night he came into our bedroom to tell us about his experience. I will never forget what he said. His words were, "Dad and Mom, I wasn't too surprised when the whole family prayed and we found my brother's hat and wallet. But this time it was just me, just me praying. I'm only sixteen and yet the Lord answered me!"

This son learned that the Lord is truly gracious to all those who will humble themselves and ask in faith. This successful experience has helped him to come to other such experiences. Now, when he needs to seek the Lord's blessings with things that are of much greater significance than a lost wallet, he knows how to ask and is learning how to ask in faith.

Testimony of Prayer

Of course, these stories aren't really about wallets and hats. I tell them to show how prayer can be a true force in our lives. In the pages that follow we will try to illustrate some principles the Lord has taught that I hope will help us to have more effective prayers. But to close this chapter, I'd like to bear my testimony that prayer really does work.

I bear testimony that the principles of receiving answers to prayer that we've seen illustrated in these stories are true principles.

I bear witness we live far below our possibilities in working with the Lord. We're too quick to turn to our own strength and not rely on him. Maybe we fear it won't work, or we fear our own inadequacies. But I bear testimony we can all learn how to utilize prayer more effectively and improve our ability to receive answers to our prayers.

I bear witness that we can learn from the Father through the Spirit of the Lord. The Father is able to communicate with his children; he does it clearly; and he does it every day. Whether we hear his promptings or not, he's still speaking to us every day—to warn us, to help us, to strengthen us, to encourage us, to fill us with joy and peace, to help us overcome obstacles and challenges.

I believe one of the primary responsibilities we have here on earth is to learn better how to hear those promptings and to hear the voice of the Lord as he speaks directly to us. Only then can we understand what he requires of us, and only then will we have the strength to be able to accomplish what he desires of us.

I believe that in the whole history of the world God has never failed to answer a humble, sincere prayer—no matter who offered it, whether male or female, young or old, weak or strong, member or nonmember. That's the way the Lord is. He is so kind. He is so anxious to respond. Of course, his answer might have been "No." Or he may have said, "Yes, but not now." Or he may have responded in a still, small voice that the person failed to hear. But answer he did, and I believe when we pass through the veil and see more clearly how prayer and revelation work, we will humbly fall upon our knees and ask the Lord's forgiveness for not more fully recognizing his hand in our lives.

Surely the Lord is anxious to respond to the petitions of his people, if they will but humbly ask in faith, be believing, and not doubt. They may then expect the arm of the Lord to be revealed in their behalf.

As Moroni testified: "As surely as Christ liveth he spake these words unto our fathers, saying: Whatsoever thing ye shall ask the Father in my name, which is good, in faith believing that ye shall receive, behold, it shall be done unto you." (Moroni 7:26.)

AN EXERCISE IN FAITH
TO SEEK A RIGHTEOUS DESIRE

Before we move to the principles that bring power in prayer, I'd like to recommend that you choose a righteous desire to seek with diligence in prayer. In the Doctrine and Covenants it says that ours is not only the only true church, but it is "the only true and *living* church upon the face of the whole earth." (D&C 1:30; italics added.) The doctrines are alive. The Lord is alive. The Spirit is alive. And so can we be if we'll be more energized and become more involved with him.

As I think about the teachings of the Church and the gospel, I feel that what makes them not only true but living is our desire and our ability to put them into practice. To me, knowledge is not nearly as important as knowledge combined with the willingness to apply it. When we learn, then, we must decide to repent, to exercise faith, and to do whatever else is required to make what we've learned operational in our lives.

Here's what I'd like you to do. Get a piece of paper and write on it something very personal that you want from the Lord—something you want very much. Don't just pick something easy. The harder it is, the better, so you can have a real experience with faith. Maybe you're concerned about your spouse. Maybe one of your children has rejected what you've taught him, and you're worried. Maybe you're struggling with a health problem. Maybe you're in the midst of great financial troubles. Maybe you just want more faith, more testimony, more strength to be able to repent and change, more ability to overcome a personal weakness. Write your desire on a piece of paper, and work on it as you proceed through this book.

Don't think you're not good enough to receive the Lord's help. As I travel around the world I meet too many members of the Church who think they can never qualify to receive answers to prayer. They say, "Sure, if I were a General Authority or the stake president or the bishop I could get answers, but I'm too . . . [fill in the blank]."

I bear witness that that's not true at all. The Lord loves all of us, and he is anxious to respond to every one of us, to help us with the righteous desires of our hearts. I've given two stories about how the Lord helped with little things, finding a hat and wallets. He truly does desire to help us in such ways—but how much more he wants to help us with the big things in our lives.

I promise you in the name of the Lord that if you really desire what you've written down, if your desire is righteous, and if you're asking *according to the will of the Lord,* he will grant you that desire—if you will learn and obey the principles and the laws that govern what you want. I have no doubt whatsoever about that. I bear testimony that it's true because the Lord has said so.

Questions to Ponder

1. In the experience of the lost hat and wallet, why did more than one person offer a prayer?

_____

_____

_____

2. What role did prayers of gratitude play in the experience of the lost hat and wallet?

_____

_____

_____

3. What role does "doing all in your power" play in receiving answers to prayer?

_____

_____

_____

4. How often does God answer our humble, sincere prayers?

_____

_____

_____

5. What makes the teachings of the gospel "true and living" to each of us?

_____

_____

_____

6. What other principles of prayer can you identify from the experience with the lost hat and wallet?

_____

_____

_____

CHAPTER 2

PREPARING YOUR HEART
AND MIND FOR PRAYER

One morning while we were living in Quito, Ecuador, I called home to tell my wife that an important guest was arriving at the airport in about an hour and that I would like to bring him home for lunch. She cheerfully said she would do her best to try to have the house clean and a nice meal prepared.

At that time we had a woman named Roza who lived with us and assisted my wife with cooking and other household chores. Roza was about thirty years old and was very strong in her own religion. We had tried repeatedly to talk to her about the Church and the gospel, but she would not listen to us at all. In fact, our attempts were usually met with a very cold reception.

That particular morning as my wife and Roza were scurrying about the kitchen trying to get the meal prepared, they discovered that Roza had lost the beater they needed to make a cake. It was a frustrating moment. In those days in Ecuador, you couldn't just make a cake from a package; you had to do it from scratch. And they didn't have the implement they needed to do it.

About this time our seven-year-old boy came into the kitchen and heard what was going on. He listened for a moment, then said to Roza, innocently, "So you lost the beater, huh?" That made her a little more angry. Then he said, "Well, if you really want to find it, why don't you ask the Lord? He knows where it is."

She answered him sharply, "You don't pray for things like that! Now get out of the kitchen so we can find it."

He hurried out, but after a few minutes she felt bad for having offended a little child and went to find him. She found him in his bedroom on his knees saying a prayer. "Heavenly Father, there is a real problem in the kitchen. Dad is bringing home an important person for lunch. Mom is upset. Roza lost the beater and she doesn't think you know where it is. If you would just show us where the beater is, the whole problem could be solved."

Within moments the lost beater was found. Some would say it was by chance, but I believe it was by faith in the Lord Jesus Christ, the faith of a little child. Roza was amazed that the Lord would answer the prayer of such a little child—and especially about something so seemingly insignificant as a beater. That experience left her with some very strong spiritual impressions about the value of prayer.

The sweetest part of this experience was that about two or three weeks later I had the privilege of baptizing Roza a member of the Church. I performed the ordinance, but a seven-year-old boy was the Lord's instrument in converting her to the truth. He taught her that whatever the problem might be, if we are really worried about it, so is the Lord. He will help us with any matter of real concern to us.

It's true that the Lord answers the prayers of little children, even in small things. It's also true that he answers the prayers of adults and that he is interested in helping us in all aspects of our lives. But our ability to receive answers to our prayers will increase as we prepare our hearts and minds to communicate with our Father in Heaven, and as we prepare ourselves, in turn, to receive from him.

Here are some important ways we can prepare our minds and hearts for prayer.

HAVE FAITH IN CHRIST

The most important thing we can do as we seek to communicate with our Heavenly Father is to have faith in Jesus Christ. If we have faith in Christ, we will have faith in our Father in Heaven, because Christ so clearly testified of him.

Some people think of faith as a positive attitude. That's only a small part of what faith really is. Faith is the power that holds the worlds in place. Faith is the power by which God works. When we have faith, we have access to his power.

But remember that the commandment is not just to have faith in a general sense. We are to have faith in a person, faith in Jesus Christ. When we seek to understand that better, we'll understand why we are to end all of our prayers "in the name of Jesus Christ." When we pray in that manner, we're asking for the grace of the Lord Jesus Christ to intervene on our behalf. If we can keep our faith centered in him it will help us to have much more power than if we pray without such faith.

When Nephi was bound with cords by his brothers, and they sought to kill him, he cried out in prayer, saying:

> O Lord, according to my faith which is in thee, wilt thou deliver me from the hands of my brethren; yea, even give me strength that I may burst these bands with which I am bound.

And it came to pass that when I had said these words, behold, the bands were loosed from off my hands and feet. (1 Nephi 7:17–18.)

Alma and Amulek had a similar experience when they, too, were bound with cords.

And Alma cried, saying: . . . O Lord, give us strength according to our faith which is in Christ, even unto deliverance. And they broke the cords with which they were bound. (Alma 14:26.)

Note that they did not have faith in their own strength; they trusted in the Lord and relied on his strength. It is faith in Christ that will deliver us from our own bonds; it is increasing our faith in Christ that will give us added power in prayer.

We can build faith by knowing:

1. God listens to our prayers and answers them. (See D&C 98:2–3; 88:2.) I believe there has not been one sincere prayer offered by any man since the "beginning" that has gone unanswered.

2. God lives and loves us and will give *correct* answers to all sincere prayers, no matter what the question is. (See Moroni 10:4–5.)

3. We are children of God and servants of the Lord. We can pray as Samuel did: "Speak; for thy servant heareth." (1 Samuel 3:10.)

4. It doesn't matter how old we are, or what our Church position is, or how long we've been members of the Church. The Lord desires to answer our sincere requests regardless of these things.

If your faith is weak, you can lean on the testimony of someone else—a parent or teacher or leader—as you seek to build your own faith.

REPENT OF YOUR SINS

Repentance is a key element in obtaining blessings from the Lord.

The story of the lost hat illustrates the need for repentance as it applies directly to the problem you're addressing in prayer. First, my son was angry at the loss of his hat and wallet, and he had to repent before we could proceed. Second, I momentarily doubted that we could find the lost items in the tall grass, and I had to repent of that feeling.

We also need to repent in other ways if we hope to qualify to receive the Lord's blessings. The more worthy we are, the more we can approach the Lord with confidence and receive answers to our prayers.

It's often not enough to simply be "temple worthy." Repentance may bring us to a state of increased fasting, more prayer, added humility, searching the scriptures, and so forth. To the degree that we are willing to change and offer up our own sins, so that the Savior can cleanse us, we can vicariously affect events and other people. If we sacrifice and pay the price, and if it is in accordance with the will of the Lord, we can receive what we righteously desire.

Part of repentance is confession, wherein we acknowledge our sins to another. Some serious sins need to be confessed to the bishop, but virtually all sins need to be confessed to the Lord. What the Lord said of Martin Harris applies to all of us:

> And now, except he humble himself and acknowledge unto me the things that he has done which are wrong, and covenant with me that he will keep my commandments, and exercise faith in me, behold, I say

unto him, he shall [not receive the blessing he seeks].
(D&C 5:28.)

HUMBLE YOURSELF BEFORE THE LORD

In the Doctrine and Covenants, the Lord directly connected humility to answered prayers when he said,

> Be thou humble; and the Lord thy God shall lead thee by the hand, and give thee answer to thy prayers. (D&C 112:10.)

When we're humble, we feel our dependency on the Lord. Because of this feeling of dependency, we reach out to him for help and guidance in many areas—and have open hearts and minds to receive it.

Some people argue that we shouldn't trouble the Lord about little things. In a way, that's a spirit of pride, a spirit of wanting to do things on one's own, rather than a desire to discover and do the Lord's will.

We hear much in the world about being self-sufficient and self-confident. We hear much about learning to do things on our own—after all, didn't the Lord bless us with good minds and the ability to think things through and reason them out on our own?

Yet that attitude takes us away from the spirit of humility and a reliance on the Lord. Certainly the Lord would have us do all that is in our power to do, but if we take the attitude of self-reliance to an extreme, we will begin to think that we can live our lives without his help.

Nephi addressed this very issue: Are there some things I ought not to pray about? Or should I pray about everything? If that's true, why don't we do it? Why is it we go on day after day, depending on our own strength?

Nephi laments about this as he talks to the brethren

of the church. After teaching them that the Holy Ghost will "show unto you all things what ye should do" (2 Nephi 32:5), he says, "And now, my beloved brethren, I perceive that ye ponder still in your hearts; and it grieveth me that I must speak concerning this thing." In other words, he says, "I hate to have to bring this up about prayer, brethren, because you already ought to know that that's the way we can receive such guidance from the Holy Ghost. It grieves me that I have to mention it to you, but I'm going to anyway because you need it."

Then he makes this significant statement:

> For if ye would hearken unto the Spirit which teacheth a man to pray ye would know that ye must pray; for the evil spirit teacheth not a man to pray, but teacheth him that he must not pray. (2 Nephi 32:8.)

The Lord wants us to grow and become strong and be able to do much good, but through it all he wants us to be dependent on the Spirit of the Lord for direction.

But Satan wants us to be dependent on him. The devil teaches us not to pray. Now that doesn't just mean nonmembers of the Church; it means he's working on each one of us: "Come on, John, you don't need to pray about that; that's too little. Don't trouble the Lord." Or, "You can handle this on your own, Mary." Or, "I know you're tired tonight, so you can skip your prayer; tomorrow will be all right. You can spend extra time in prayer tomorrow." And thus does the devil whisper to us, because the evil spirit teacheth a man not to pray. At the same time, the Holy Spirit is teaching us to pray.

Now consider the next verse: "But behold, I say unto you that ye must pray always, and not faint." When should I pray? Pray always! "Ye must not perform anything"—what's the word? Anything!

> Ye must not perform any thing unto the Lord save in
> the first place ye shall pray unto the Father in the name
> of Christ, that he will consecrate thy performance unto
> thee, that thy performance may be for the welfare of
> thy soul. (2 Nephi 32:9.)

That's not just talking about praying before we do
our Church work. We should pray for guidance, direction, and blessing about every aspect of our lives. As
Alma taught:

> Cry unto God for all thy support; yea, let all thy doings
> be unto the Lord, and whithersoever thou goest let it
> be in the Lord; yea, let all thy thoughts be directed unto
> the Lord; yea, let the affections of thy heart be placed
> upon the Lord forever.
>   Counsel with the Lord in all thy doings, and he will
> direct thee for good. (Alma 37:36–37.)

There's a lot in those verses. The Lord knows that
there are things we could do on our own if we so desired.
(Although on a deeper level we can't do anything on our
own, because we belong to him, the air we breathe
belongs to him—everything about our lives is a gift from
God.) But the Lord says, "I understand that you can do
many things on your own, but if you want your actions
to be for your spiritual well-being, you must pray and
consecrate them unto me." Sometimes the purpose of
such a prayer is simply to check in with Him, to tell him
what you're planning to do, and to ask for his blessings.
But at the same time, we should ask for instructions and
guidance: Am I on the right course? Is there anything
thou wouldst desire me to change about what I'm going
to do? Is it all pleasing? Is there another approach that
would be better?

There is always a danger in stressing so fervently

these ideas about our being totally dependent upon the Lord. For some, it is all too easy to become fanatical; some feel that they should be on their knees praying all the time when instead they should be out working, having prayed already and continuing to pray in their hearts.

Some people expect the Lord to do all the work and reveal things to them that they haven't bothered to study out in their minds beforehand (see D&C 9). Some become extreme and perhaps say, rather pridefully, "I prayed through the entire night the last two nights; I didn't sleep at all," or "I fasted for three days straight." Or a young returned missionary might say, "I've been waiting for a wife now for five years. I've been praying and praying, but the Lord still hasn't sent her to me. I haven't done much dating, but I'm sure that when the Lord finds her, he will have her come and find me."

Others may be paralyzed into inaction, waiting for an answer from the heavens, when in actuality the Lord may be requiring them to move ahead, proceeding the best way they know how, before he will confirm their course.

Brigham Young once said:

> If I do not know the will of my Father, and what He requires of me in a certain transaction, if I ask Him to give me wisdom concerning any requirement in life, or in regard to my own course, or that of my friends, my family, my children, or those that I preside over, and get no answer from Him, and then do the very best that my judgment will teach me, He is bound to own and honor that transaction, and He will do so to all intents and purposes. (*Journal of Discourses*, 3:205.)

As we acknowledge our dependence on the Lord, we increase in our humility—and we enhance our ability to truly communicate with the Lord. Those who truly are humble will also do all in their power to do their part, knowing that answers to prayer are a mutual endeavor, requiring effort by both man and God.

Obey the Commandments

King Benjamin taught:

> I would desire that ye should consider on the blessed and happy state of those that keep the commandments of God. For behold, they are blessed in all things, both temporal and spiritual. (Mosiah 2:41.)

The more we keep the commandments, the more we'll be able to receive the blessings of the Lord, including answers to prayer.

This connection between obedience and obtaining answers to prayer is clearly taught in the scriptures. I'll give you just two examples:

> If ye will not harden your hearts, and ask me in faith, believing that ye shall receive, with diligence in keeping my commandments, surely these things shall be made known unto you. (1 Nephi 15:11.)

> Whatsoever we ask, we receive of him, because we keep his commandments, and do those things that are pleasing in his sight. (1 John 3:22.)

Be Willing to Sacrifice

Blessings usually don't come for free. In return the Lord typically requires obedience and sacrifice. We must "sacrifice, pay the price."

Most sacrifice comes in the form of repentance—we give up the sins and bad habits that we so much want to cling to. But when we give them up, we're greatly blessed, not only in getting rid of the sins but also in an increased influence of the Spirit in our lives.

The sacrifice of repentance is part of what the Lord was referring to when he said,

> Thou shalt offer a sacrifice unto the Lord thy God in righteousness, even that of a broken heart and a contrite spirit. (D&C 59:8.)

Sacrifice truly can increase the power of our prayers, if we will consecrate that sacrifice to the Lord. Suppose, for example, you are a mother or father with a son who is straying from the path of righteousness. I believe you can do much to pray him home. You can do much to fast him home. You can repent enough of your own sins that, through your sacrifice, the Lord may intervene more in his life and save the boy. It's not that you're paying for your own sins—Jesus did that. But through your agency, through your sacrifice, you are able to receive blessings that you otherwise would not be able to obtain. (Of course, these things still depend on the agency of others—our prayers can't supersede the agency of those we're praying for. But sacrifice and fervent prayer can do much to help. With such prayer we can accomplish much—even if it doesn't bring our loved ones all the way home. Without such prayer, we're lost.)

One must also remember to always pray to be subject to the will of the Lord in all things. The Lord's will certainly will always be done. We can list all of these keys to improving our prayers, elements over which we have some control, but we must always remember that, in spite of our desires and in spite of diligent efforts to do our part, the Lord's will is the final controlling factor.

Increase Your Desire

The Lord has said that he would grant unto us according to our desires. (See, for example, Enos 1:12; Alma 9:20; 18:35; 29:5; 41:3–5; D&C 11:17.) As we prepare our minds and hearts for prayer, we can increase our desire to talk to the Lord, we can seek more fully to align our desires with those of God, and we can desire more fully to receive answers from him.

When the Nephite disciples were praying in the presence of Jesus, "they did not multiply many words, for it was given unto them what they should pray, and they were filled with desire." (3 Nephi 19:24.)

And the Lord has promised in our day:

> Behold, according to your desires, yea, even according to your faith shall it be done unto you. (D&C 11:17.)

These promises can be ours, if we will seek for them.

Part of being able to grow in desire is to be sincere in our seeking. We earlier noted the promise of the Lord to Martin Harris:

> If he will bow down before me, and humble himself in mighty prayer and faith, in the sincerity of his heart, then will I grant unto him a view of the things which he desires to see. (D&C 5:24.)

Moroni also emphasized the need for sincerity in prayer when he said,

> Ask God . . . if these things are not true; and if ye shall ask with a sincere heart, with real intent, having faith in Christ, he will manifest the truth of it unto you. (Moroni 10:4.)

Eliminate Anger and Contention from Your Heart

When my son wanted help with finding his hat and wallet, I knew we couldn't help him through prayer because he was too angry. You simply cannot get answers to prayer when you have anger in your heart. But after he had spent some time on his knees humbling himself and letting the Lord remove the anger from within him, then he was ready for us to try to help him seek the answer he desired.

Of course, this principle is true not only of anger but of all the negative emotions—lust, jealousy, covetousness, contention, revenge, bitterness, doubt, and so forth.

Discipline Your Mind

Jacob spoke of the blessing that comes with discipline of mind in prayer:

> I, Jacob, would speak unto you that are pure in heart. Look unto God with firmness of mind, and pray unto him with exceeding faith, and he will console you in your afflictions, and he will plead your cause, and send down justice upon those who seek your destruction. (Jacob 3:1.)

The Lord counseled Oliver Cowdery that he would have more success at receiving inspiration to translate the Book of Mormon if he would first "study it out in [his] mind." (D&C 9:8.) Concentrating the mind on a problem helps to open us to the inspiration of the Lord.

James, in the New Testament, adds his testimony about the importance of a proper mental focus when it comes to answers to prayer:

> If any of you lack wisdom, let him ask of God, that

giveth to all men liberally, and upbraideth not; and it shall be given him.

But let him ask in faith, nothing wavering. For he that wavereth is like a wave of the sea driven with the wind and tossed.

For let not that man think that he shall receive any thing of the Lord.

A double minded man is unstable in all his ways. (James 1:5–8.)

Focusing and concentrating the mind on your prayer, and on the blessing you seek, is an important exercise of agency that helps you to qualify for the Lord's blessings. Such concentration is part of faith, and faith is essential to receiving answers to prayer.

Preparing the heart and the mind for the Lord's answers blesses us in two important ways:

First, it helps to qualify us for the blessing we seek. The Lord honors us when we seek to be righteous, both without and within, and he desires to answer our prayers and help us with our problems.

Second, as we turn our hearts and minds to the Lord, we're more able to receive the answers he sends. The Lord said through Joseph Smith:

Behold, I will tell you in your mind and in your heart, by the Holy Ghost, which shall come upon you and which shall dwell in your heart.

Now, behold, this is the spirit of revelation. (D&C 8:2–3.)

King Limhi told his people that they would receive the blessings they sought from the Lord if they would "turn to the Lord with full purpose of heart, and put [their] trust in him, and serve him with all diligence of mind." (Mosiah 7:33.)

So will it be with us. If we hope to receive answers to our prayers, as my sweet little son did in the story of the lost beater, we must first prepare our hearts and our minds.

RECEIVING ANSWERS QUICKLY

Before we conclude this chapter, I want to answer a question I'm often asked: Is there something that governs the rapidity with which the Lord answers?

Hidden behind the question is the observation that the Lord seems to answer the prayers of some people immediately, while others have to struggle for a long time.

I feel a good answer to this question can be found in Doctrine and Covenants 101:

> They were slow to hearken unto the voice of the Lord their God; therefore, the Lord their God is slow to hearken unto their prayers, to answer them in the day of their trouble.
>
> In the day of their peace they esteemed lightly my counsel; but, in the day of their trouble, of necessity they feel after me. (Vv. 7–8.)

These verses are a lament from the Lord, a lament that most of us don't really get serious about something until we are in a dire emergency. Then we beg the Lord for help.

And he's saying, in essence, "Where were you when things were going better? Why didn't you come then?"

I believe that when we're slow to hearken unto the voice of the Lord, the Lord is slow to hearken unto our prayers and to answer us in the day of our trouble.

Of course, even if in the past we've been slow to turn to God, we can repent. As the Lord continues:

Verily I say unto you, notwithstanding their sins, my bowels are filled with compassion towards them. (D&C 101:9.)

I believe that if you want to increase the rapidity with which the Lord responds to you, you need to increase the rapidity with which you respond to the voice of the Spirit.

There is a second requirement: We can't respond begrudgingly. "The Lord requireth the heart and a willing mind"; he requires that we not only be "obedient" but that we also be "willing." (D&C 64:34.) He requires further that we receive all his gifts with gratitude—even those gifts that seem to be trials:

Ye are commanded in all things to ask of God, who giveth liberally; and that which the Spirit testifies unto you even so I would that ye should do in all holiness of heart, walking uprightly before me, considering the end of your salvation, doing all things with prayer and thanksgiving. (D&C 46:7.)

Finally, if we want the Lord to respond quickly, we must be humble. Doctrine and Covenants 112 contains these beautiful words: "Be thou humble; and the Lord thy God shall lead thee by the hand, and give thee answer to thy prayers." (V. 10.) What a great jewel! If you are humble, he will lead you by the hand to show you what sacrifice is needed, and then he will give you an answer to your prayers.

But we must remember in all this that even if the Lord answers quickly, his answer may not always be "yes." According to his wisdom and his will, he may answer "no," or "maybe later."

In essence, then, the thing that usually determines our ability to receive answers quickly is ourselves—our own hearts and minds. When our hearts and minds are pure, when they're turned to the Lord, and when we're trying to apply the principles discussed in this chapter, we will learn how to increase our ability to get answers more quickly and clearly.

Questions to Ponder

1. Why is it so important to prepare your heart and mind before prayer?

_____

_____

_____

2. What are some key ways we can build faith?

_____

_____

_____

3. Why is repentance such an important key to obtaining blessings from the Lord?

_____

_____

_____

4. According to the teachings of Nephi, are there some things about which we ought not to pray? Or should we pray about everything? Why?

_____

_____

_____

5. Who teaches us not to pray? Why?

_____

_____

_____

6. What is the danger of stressing the truth that we are totally dependent upon the Lord? How can we be dependent without falling into that danger?

_____

_____

_____

7. What did Brigham Young teach we should do if we ask the Lord for guidance and receive no answer?

_____

_____

_____

8. When we seek blessings, we usually have to give something in return. What is most often required?

_____

_____

_____

9. What form does most sacrifice take?

_____

_____

_____

10. How can we grow in proper desires?

_____

_____

_____

11. Why is it not possible to hear the Lord's answers when we're filled with anger or any of the other negative emotions?

_____

_____

_____

12. What determines whether we receive answers quickly or not? (Ask yourself: What can I improve upon to receive answers more quickly in my life?)

_____

_____

_____

CHAPTER 3

SOME SUGGESTIONS REGARDING THE PRACTICE OF PRAYER

If we have prepared our hearts and minds for prayer, the Lord will hear and bless us. The state of our hearts is of greater importance than the actual approach we use.

Still, our blessings will increase if we will pray in the manner the Lord has prescribed. Let me share with you a few vital elements in the practice of prayer.

ADDRESS GOD AS OUR FATHER

In the Lord's Prayer, Jesus said we should begin by saying "Our Father which art in heaven." (Matt. 6:9.)

In a meeting in Kirtland, Ohio, Heber C. Kimball related an experience with his daughter that demonstrated the sweet power of addressing our Father in faith:

"My wife, one day, when going out on a visit, gave my daughter Helen Mar charge not to touch the dishes, for if she broke any during her absence she would give her a whipping when she returned. While my wife was absent my daughter broke a number of the dishes by letting the table leaf fall, and then she went out under an apple tree and prayed that her mother's heart might be softened, that when she returned she might not whip her. Her mother was very punctual when she

34

made a promise to her children, to fulfill it, and when she returned she undertook, as a duty, to carry this promise into effect. She retired with her into her room, but found herself powerless to chastise her; her heart was so softened that it was impossible for her to raise her hand against the child. Afterwards, Helen told her mother she had prayed to the Lord that she might not whip her."

Heber paused in his simple narrative. Tears glistened in the eyes of his hearers. The Prophet Joseph was weeping like a child. He told the brethren that that was the kind of faith they needed—the faith of a little child, going in humility to its Parent, and asking for the desire of its heart. (Orson F. Whitney, *The Life of Heber C. Kimball* [Salt Lake City: Bookcraft, 1945], p. 69.)

We've had a similar experience in our own family. One day I arrived home from work to find my youngest son in a very sober mood. Looking extremely sad, he put his arms around me, then asked me to go with him into the bedroom.

There lying on the bed was my backyard thermometer along with about seven dollars in bills and coins—all the money he had. He told me through his tears that he was really sorry, but he had accidentally broken the thermometer by kicking his ball into it. To make matters worse, he had broken the front-yard thermometer just a week before. (I had been able to fix that one.) He knew that I had taken some trouble to calibrate the two thermometers so they worked together to measure the temperatures in different locations, and that I had calibrated them with the indoor thermostat as well. He was absolutely certain I was going to be really upset.

I put my arm around him and told him I forgave him. He was so repentant I didn't have the heart to make him pay for it, even though that is what I would normally have done.

Later that evening he told me that that morning he had prayed fervently to the Lord that his dad would not be angry with him. He knew his prayer had been answered.

A subsequent experience the next morning made all this extra sweet. As we read scriptures as a family, we began to talk about how the Spirit comes to us and blesses us. I asked the children, "When was the last time you really felt like the Spirit helped you?" This youngest son answered, with great feeling, "Just yesterday."

Then he told me that after I'd left the room the previous night, he had offered a second prayer. He had knelt down and thanked the Lord with all his heart for answering his prayer and helping his dad to not be upset with him. He said, "I really feel like the Spirit inspired me and that I was able to get my prayer answered. I'm glad I told the Lord I was thankful."

I'm thankful that we can go to our Father in simplicity, as shown in these stories and in the Lord's Prayer. He's not there to hear flowery words; he wants to hear in simple words from your heart what you're feeling. And if you recognize him to be your Father in Heaven and talk to him that way (and I put emphasis on your *Father*), you'll have much more power in your prayers.

PRAY IN THE NAME OF JESUS CHRIST

Jesus is our Lord and Savior. He is our advocate with the Father. We should do all that we do in his name. This has been the rule of God from the beginning. As an angel taught Adam,

Thou shalt do all that thou doest in the name of the

Son, and thou shalt repent and call upon God in the name of the Son forevermore. (Moses 5:8.)

Nephi reiterated this principle:

Ye must not perform any thing unto the Lord save in the first place ye shall pray unto the Father in the name of Christ. (2 Nephi 32:9.)

The Lord taught the same thing to his disciples when he was on the earth:

Whatsoever ye shall ask in my name, that will I do, that the Father may be glorified in the Son.
If ye shall ask any thing in my name, I will do it. (John 14:13–14.)

These are the fundamentals of prayer: To pray with a true heart and mind, to address the Father, and to pray in the name of Jesus Christ. If we will do these things, all else will fall into place.

But there is more we ought to consider. Here are some additional aspects of the practice of prayer you should keep in mind:

FIND A STILL PLACE

The Lord said to Oliver Cowdery:

If you desire a further witness, cast your mind upon the night that you cried unto me in your heart, that you might know concerning the truth of these things.
Did I not speak peace to your mind concerning the matter? (D&C 6:22–23.)

The Lord usually speaks to us in quiet whisperings. If we are not in a quiet, still place when we approach him, we might not hear (or feel) his answers.

KNEEL DOWN

Kneeling, where possible, shows our humility and dependence on the Lord. It shows that we recognize his greatness and our "nothingness," as King Benjamin put it. (See Mosiah 4:11.)

We have already quoted the Lord's condemnation and promise to Martin Harris:

> He exalts himself and does not humble himself sufficiently before me; but if he will bow down before me, and humble himself in mighty prayer and faith, in the sincerity of his heart, then will I grant unto him a view of the things which he desires to see. (D&C 5:24.)

PONDER AND STUDY THINGS OUT IN YOUR MIND

When it comes to prayer and revelation, our minds need to be active and engaged if we hope to receive answers from the Lord. If we simply wait passively for something to come into our empty minds, we'll wait a long time. The Lord requires us to use our agency as an important prerequisite to receiving answers to prayer. Pondering and studying things out in our minds is part of that process.

The Lord said to Oliver Cowdery:

> Behold, you have not understood; you have supposed that I would give it unto you, when you took no thought save it was to ask me.
>
> But, behold, I say unto you, that you must study it out in your mind; then you must ask me if it be right, and if it is right I will cause that your bosom shall burn within you; therefore, you shall feel that it is right.
>
> But if it be not right you shall have no such feelings, but you shall have a stupor of thought that shall cause

you to forget the thing which is wrong; therefore, you cannot write that which is sacred save it be given you from me. (D&C 9:7–9.)

As you can see from this declaration of the Lord, he doesn't want us to just ask him, assuming that he will solve all of our problems. That would make us dependent and weak. Instead, he wants us to be a party to solving our problems, and thus we must think it out, ponder it, perhaps seek counsel from others, and then ask the Lord to confirm our decision or direction.

The Lord also makes it clear that if the direction or decision we have made is not right, he will give us a stupor of thought, which will cause us to forget that direction or decision we were pursuing. If something is not right and you will wait a little while, many times in a few days you will have feelings that are exactly opposite from those you previously had, and you thereby will have an answer to your prayer.

ASK!

The Lord rarely gives us answers to questions we don't ask. He rarely grants requests we don't seek.

Jesus taught this principle when he was on the earth. He said:

> Ask, and it shall be given you; seek, and ye shall find; knock, and it shall be opened unto you:
>
> For every one that asketh receiveth; and he that seeketh findeth; and to him that knocketh it shall be opened.
>
> Or what man is there of you, whom if his son ask bread, will he give him a stone?
>
> Or if he ask a fish, will he give him a serpent?
>
> If ye then, being evil, know how to give good gifts

unto your children, how much more shall your Father
which is in heaven give good things to them that ask
him? (Matthew 7:7–11.)

The scriptures are filled with this promise. If you
want to have a good exercise in seeing how fully the
Lord promises us answers if we will ask, see James 4:2–3;
2 Nephi 32:4; 3 Nephi 27:28–29; and Doctrine and
Covenants 6:5, 42:68, and 103:31.

But there are some conditions. We must be "believing" (Matthew 21:22; Enos 1:15); we must "abide" in
Christ, and let his words abide in us (John 15:7); we must
"keep his commandments, and do those things that are
pleasing in his sight" (1 John 3:22); we must ask "according to his will" (1 John 5:14); we must "ask not amiss" (2
Nephi 4:35); we must ask that which "is right" (Mosiah
4:21; 3 Nephi 18:20); we must "[believe] in Christ, doubt-
ing nothing" (Mormon 9:21); we must ask that "which is
good, in faith believing that [we] shall receive" (Moroni
7:26); and we must ask for those things that are "expedient" for us (D&C 88:64).

Nephi gives a good summary of these requirements:

If ye will not harden your hearts, and ask me in faith,
believing that ye shall receive, with diligence in keeping my commandments, surely these things shall be
made known unto you. (1 Nephi 15:11.)

Asking is so important that even the restoration of the
gospel hinged upon it. Here is Joseph Smith's account of
how his asking led to the First Vision—and all else that
followed:

While I was laboring under the extreme difficulties
caused by the contests of these parties of religionists, I
was one day reading the Epistle of James, first chapter

and fifth verse, which reads: *If any of you lack wisdom, let him ask of God, that giveth to all men liberally, and upbraideth not; and it shall be given him.*

Never did any passage of scripture come with more power to the heart of man than this did at this time to mine. It seemed to enter with great force into every feeling of my heart. I reflected on it again and again, knowing that if any person needed wisdom from God, I did. . . .

At length I came to the conclusion that I must either remain in darkness and confusion, or else I must do as James directs, that is, *ask* of God. I at length came to the determination to *"ask* of God," concluding that if he gave wisdom to them that lacked wisdom, and would give liberally, and not upbraid, I might venture.

So, in accordance with this, my determination to *ask* of God, I retired to the woods to make the attempt. It was on the morning of a beautiful, clear day, early in the spring of eighteen hundred and twenty. (Joseph Smith–History 1:11–14; emphasis added.)

After the heavens had opened, and God had poured forth his light of truth, Joseph recorded,

I had found the testimony of James to be true—that a man who lacked wisdom might *ask* of God, and obtain, and not be upbraided. (Joseph Smith–History 1:26; emphasis added.)

My experience with many members is that they struggle for answers not because they're unworthy or fail to measure up, but because they don't ask—or they ask once or twice and give up, without really persisting and pleading with the Lord for an answer. Certainly personal worthiness is part of it, as we have discussed. But the promise is there: if we will ask with a sincere heart, we will receive.

As you struggle with feelings of unworthiness, then, feeling you're not good enough or that you don't measure up, remember that the Lord doesn't require us to be perfect or near perfect before he'll give us answers to prayers. He wants to give us answers to help us along that long path to perfection. But he does require us to ask—and not just to ask once and be done with it, but to ask over and over again, with true desire and persistence.

Let us also remember that there is a significant difference between asking the Lord for knowledge and asking him to intervene in life's events or circumstances like the weather, illness, the behavior of other individuals, and so forth.

On the one hand, the Lord has promised numerous times that he is waiting to pour out knowledge on the heads of the Latter-day Saints. In this instance, there seem to be few barriers to one's receiving answers if he will just humble himself and ask.

On the other hand, to ask the Lord to change events or circumstances involving one's self or others is much more complicated, because there are so many variables. In the case of trying to alter circumstances (the weather, one's trials, events in life), it may be that many of those circumstances or events were decreed to serve purposes of the Lord that are unknown to you.

In the case of praying to alter the conduct of another, the agency of that person must be honored, or perhaps the Lord has an individualized curriculum underway for his development, or others are being influenced or blessed as a result of praying for him, and so forth.

Because of all that is unknown to us, when we are asking the Lord to change events or circumstances we would do well to truly pray and always rely on the Lord that he will do what is best for all concerned.

Use Prayer Language

God is pleased when we show respect to him by using formal prayer language. Instead of using the overly familiar "you," "your," and so forth, we should use the language of the scriptures: "thee," "thine," and so forth.

Some people are uncomfortable with this kind of language, feeling they can't use it well. But the more we pray that way and learn that kind of respectful language by immersing ourselves in the scriptures, the more we're able to use it in our prayers.

> After this manner therefore pray ye: Our Father which art in heaven, Hallowed be thy name. (Matthew 6:9.)

Don't Multiply Words

When the Nephite disciples were praying in the presence of Jesus, they set a good example for us all. The record says,

> They did still continue, without ceasing, to pray unto him; and they did not multiply many words, for it was given unto them what they should pray, and they were filled with desire. (3 Nephi 19:24.)

This is consistent with the commandment the Lord gave to the Jews during his mortal ministry. He said, "When ye pray, use not vain repetitions, as the heathen do: for they think that they shall be heard for their much speaking." (Matthew 6:7; also see 3 Nephi 13:7.)

When we pray publicly, let us be careful to never be swept away in the desire for the honors of men, which might cause us to pray without real intent or to unnecessarily extend the length of our prayers. The same caution applies to those who pray for a mortal audience rather than simply to be heard by the Lord. We must always be careful to avoid "flowery" prayers or prayers to impress. Surely the Lord is not pleased with such an approach, nor will he answer the prayers of one who is not focused on the Lord or who prays without real intent.

PRAY VOCALLY

The Lord said something to Martin Harris that applies to all of us:

> I command thee that thou shalt pray vocally as well as in thy heart; yea, before the world as well as in secret, in public as well as in private. (D&C 19:28.)

There's something powerful in vocal prayer. It helps to concentrate our thoughts and focus our feelings.

Some of the most significant prayers we have on record were vocal prayers. Of the Lord's great intercessory prayer, uttered just before he entered the Garden of Gethsemane, John says, "These words spake Jesus." (John 17:1.) We have some of the words Jesus spoke in the Garden, indicating that at least some of that prayer was vocal. (See Matthew 26:39–44.) When Jesus was among the Nephites, he prayed aloud, using words that "cannot be written." (3 Nephi 17:15.)

It appears others may have also prayed vocally. Nephi wrote, "By day have I waxed bold in mighty prayer before him; yea, my voice have I sent up on high." (2 Nephi 4:24.) Enos said,

> I kneeled down before my Maker, and I cried unto him in mighty prayer and supplication for mine own soul; and all the day long did I cry unto him; yea, and when the night came I did still raise my voice high that it reached the heavens. (Enos 1:4.)

Nephi, son of Helaman, went into a tower in his garden to pray, which prayer was heard by passers-by. (See Helaman 7:6–11.) When Alma and his people were in bondage to the Lamanites, they cried out unto God for deliverance, until guards were assigned to kill all those who prayed aloud. (See Mosiah 24:10–12.)

Finally, Joseph Smith prayed vocally in the Sacred Grove, opening the door to the great restoration of the gospel in this last dispensation of time. (See Joseph Smith–History 1:14.)

As important as these instructions are regarding vocal prayer, the Lord also consistently teaches about secret prayer. Sometimes it may only be a thought, a feeling, or an expression of gratitude, but these can be effective prayers as well. A prayer can be something as simple as an utterance in your heart—"Heavenly Father, please help me" or "Speak, Lord, thy servant heareth"—knowing that the Lord truly answers that kind of prayer too. The Lord said to Oliver Cowdery:

> Thou hast inquired of me, and behold, as often as thou hast inquired thou hast received instruction of my Spirit. . . .
>
> Behold, thou knowest that thou hast inquired of me and I did enlighten thy mind; and now I tell thee these things that thou mayest know that thou hast been enlightened by the Spirit of truth;
>
> Yea, I tell thee, that thou mayest know that there is none else save God that knowest thy thoughts and the intents of thy heart. (D&C 6:14–16.)

It is evident here that Oliver Cowdery had inquired of the Lord and had not realized that he had received an answer. The Lord then reveals that he knew Oliver had prayed to him and that he had answered his prayer. He also made it clear that only God knows the thoughts and intents of one's heart.

There are many times when it is appropriate to pray silently, and there are other times when we'll want to pray vocally. Whatever our practice, over the years the prophets have taught that at least twice a day, morning and evening, we should find a private place, kneel down, and pour out our hearts to our Father in Heaven. Then, throughout the day, we can do our best to keep a prayer in our hearts. As we do, if our hearts are right, we will find that our prayers have increased power and focus, and we'll discover that we're in a better position to receive answers.

PRAY REPEATEDLY

The Lord doesn't like vain repetitions, but when we're praying from the heart, our requests are not "vain," even if they're often repeated.

When we were trying to find my son's hat and wallet, we felt it was appropriate to approach the Lord repeatedly. We had a prayer together, then prayed again after we'd reached the field. As we rode we kept a prayer in our hearts. After we'd found the lost items, we offered a prayer of thanksgiving.

Right after the Lord taught us how to pray in the Lord's prayer, he gave us a parable that helps us understand this idea. He said:

> Which of you shall have a friend, and shall go unto him at midnight, and say unto him, Friend, lend me three loaves;
> For a friend of mine in his journey is come to me, and I have nothing to set before him?
> And he from within shall answer and say, Trouble

me not: the door is now shut, and my children are with me in bed; I cannot rise and give thee.

I say unto you, Though he will not rise and give him, because he is his friend, yet because of his importunity he will rise and give him as many as he needeth.

And I say unto you, Ask, and it shall be given you; seek, and ye shall find; knock, and it shall be opened unto you. (Luke 11:5–9.)

The Lord is saying here that we can approach our Father in Heaven repeatedly on the same thing. By doing so, we show that we are sincere and filled with desire. Some might be concerned that in this process we might overly repeat ourselves. The Lord knows we are going to ask for many of the same things over the years in our prayers, perhaps even in many of the same words. That is not the problem. In my judgment, repetition is a problem only when we're using it without real intent, just saying words—then it's called vain repetition, which the Lord condemns.

LISTEN FOR ANSWERS

Since the Lord usually speaks in a still, small voice, we often won't hear his answers unless we take the time to listen. I believe the best prayers are often filled with spaces of silence—we're not only talking to our Father, but we're also listening to his responses. Then, when the prayer is over, we can continue to seek feelings and answers by remaining on our knees for a few moments before we move on with the concerns of the day.

Questions to Ponder

1. What are some of the most basic fundamentals of prayer?

_____

_____

_____

2. Why is it helpful to find a quiet, still place to pray?

_____

_____

_____

3. What is the symbolism of kneeling before the Lord?

_____

_____

_____

4. Why does the Lord often require us to study things out in our minds as part of our preparation to receive answers to prayer?

_____

_____

_____

5. Even if they're worthy, many members still struggle for answers to prayers. Why?

_____

_____

_____

6. Why is it important to persist in prayer and not give up easily?

_____

_____

_____

7. What are the advantages of vocal prayer and silent prayer?

_____

_____

_____

CHAPTER 4

PRINCIPLES THAT ADD POWER TO YOUR PRAYERS

Not too long ago one of our sons wrote home from his mission and told us of a sweet experience he'd had with prayer.

He was riding his bike in the dark behind his companion somewhere in the Pachuca, Mexico, area. They were late for a discussion. He said, "As we were racing through the dark, I felt impressed to pray. I did so, offering a prayer of gratitude for being a missionary, for being in Mexico, for being able to serve the Lamanites. I tried my best to express my thanks to the Lord.

"Right in the middle of the prayer, I felt the Spirit say to me, 'Put your other hand on the handlebars.' (As you remember, I always ride with one hand.) I obeyed, and within a matter of seconds, the bike nearly crashed into a deep hole in the middle of the road. Because I was using two hands, I was able to swerve the bike around the hole and continue safely."

He might have been seriously hurt, but instead he was uninjured. He drew two important conclusions from this incident. He said, "I have been constantly reminded how *quiet* the voice of the Spirit is. It is so quiet that if you are not quiet you will not hear it." He also testified, "I believe if I had not been praying at that very moment, I would not have heard the voice. Because I was praying, I heard."

We're better able to hear the Spirit's voice when we're being constant in prayer; and when we recognize and obey that voice, we receive more power in prayer.

I believe, then, that we learn to hear the Spirit better when we learn how to pray without ceasing. I feel we need to learn to pray our way through each day, to pray over big things and little things, to just check in, just have a conversation, let the Lord know what we're feeling and what we're doing.

But that's not the end of it. We then should be open to any direction he desires to give us. Sometimes that direction will flow in impressive ways; sometimes we may not receive much. But we always need to be open to it.

I would like to emphasize that to the degree that you learn to really pray without ceasing—to have your heart drawn out to the Lord and to let your heart be broken and your spirit contrite—to that same degree you establish an environment where the Lord can speak directly to you and you can hear his voice.

The Lord wants us to be a prayerful friend to him on good days as well as bad days. We must attempt to "look unto [God] in every thought." (D&C 6:36.)

This is a great principle in prayer: to recognize our dependence on God, and to constantly seek his power and blessing in our lives. In this chapter, we'll talk about that principle of prayer and a number of others as well.

RECOGNIZE YOUR DEPENDENCE ON THE LORD

It seems that most of us to try to solve our problems on our own, with our own strength. Yet the Lord has truly commanded us to pray over all things:

Therefore may God grant unto you, my brethren, that ye may begin to exercise your faith unto repentance, that ye begin to call upon his holy name, that he would have mercy upon you;

Yea, cry unto him for mercy; for he is mighty to save.

Yea, humble yourselves, and continue in prayer unto him.

Cry unto him when ye are in your fields, yea, over all your flocks.

Cry unto him in your houses, yea, over all your household, both morning, mid-day, and evening.

Yea, cry unto him against the power of your enemies.

Yea, cry unto him against the devil, who is an enemy to all righteousness.

Cry unto him over the crops of your fields, that ye may prosper in them.

Cry over the flocks of your fields, that they may increase.

But this is not all; ye must pour out your souls in your closets, and your secret places, and in your wilderness.

Yea, and when you do not cry unto the Lord, let your hearts be full, drawn out in prayer unto him continually for your welfare, and also for the welfare of those who are around you. (Alma 34:17–27.)

There seems to be no question that we are to pray over all things. As the Lord has said in this dispensation,

Ye are commanded in all things to ask of God, who giveth liberally; and that which the Spirit testifies unto you even so I would that ye should do in all holiness of heart, walking uprightly before me, considering the end of your salvation, doing all things with prayer and thanksgiving. (D&C 46:7.)

I have a feeling that many of us go through our days trying to resolve our own problems—spiritual, temporal, and otherwise—and do not turn to the Lord as we should. We can receive all sorts of blessings from the Lord, but we must ask, we must ask in faith, and we must know that we are utterly dependent on the Lord for all our support.

PRAY WITHOUT CEASING

"Pray always, that you may come off conqueror," the Lord has said, "yea, that you may conquer Satan." (D&C 10:5.)

In that great sermon on prayer we've just quoted, Amulek reminds us, "When you do not cry unto the Lord, let your hearts be full, drawn out in prayer unto him continually." (Alma 34:27.)

When our hearts are constantly turned to the Lord, we more fully open the channel between us and him, which helps us to be more receptive to his answers to our prayers.

PRAY FERVENTLY

James wrote: "The effectual fervent prayer of a righteous man availeth much." (James 5:16.) And Moroni promised that our prayers would be answered if we "ask with a sincere heart, with real intent, having faith in Christ." (Moroni 10:4.)

When we pray with fervency we pray with real intent. We pray from the heart. We really mean what we say, and we say what we feel. This brings an added humility, an increased power to our prayers that we never have when we pray in a surface manner only, perhaps only speaking words.

BE SPECIFIC IN YOUR REQUESTS

The Lord will be involved in the *specifics* of your life if you invite him to be. In my own life, I've seen time and again how true this is. I may be struggling with a problem and trying all sorts of solutions. Then, after the frustration that usually comes from relying on my own strength, I finally humble myself and ask for help in a specific way. I testify that consistently the Lord gives me ideas or thoughts or feelings that help me to come to the resolution of the problem. I am surely thankful for a loving, gracious Father in Heaven, who will answer prayers and do so immediately.

I bear testimony that the problem with most of us is that we do not ask specifically enough or perhaps with the strength of real intent. How much the Lord wants to bless us, and yet many of us will not ask.

I further bear testimony that the Lord does answer the prayers of his children, when they are offered in faith. He will answer on any issue that is of concern to us, because of his great love for each of his children. May each of us pray more specifically and with real intent that the heavens may more effectively respond to us.

CAST OUT DOUBT AND FEAR

I'm always impressed as I think of the negative power of doubt and fear on the power of faith. Joseph Smith said, in essence, "Doubt and fear cannot reside in the mind of man at the same time as faith. One or the other will leave." (See N. B. Lundwall, comp., *Lectures on Faith* [Salt Lake City, n.d.], lecture 4, paragraph 13.)

One of the greatest difficulties of trying to accomplish something through faith and prayer is to really believe it will happen. Doubt and fear are so powerful that they can sometimes dissuade you from starting the endeavor in the first place, or when you get started they can motivate you to quit.

We all know the story of Peter walking on the water. He saw Jesus approaching them on the surface of the sea, and, in a great act of faith, said, "Bid me come unto thee." (Matthew 14:28.) Jesus bade him to come, and Peter stepped out of the boat. You can imagine his feelings as he put all his weight on his foot and started to step into the Sea of Galilee. Then all of a sudden he was walking, the second man in the history of the world (as far as we know) to walk on water! Then it appears the devil moved into the picture. The wind stirred up, and waves lifted higher, and Peter began to doubt; he was filled with fear; and down he went into that dark, frightening water.

Then Jesus reached out and saved him, saying, "O thou of little faith, wherefore didst thou doubt?" (Matthew 14:31.) Jesus could also have added, "Peter, you were tied to my power, as long as you were believing and walking and having faith. But the moment you let doubt in, see what happens?"

What a great lesson! And how essential! I'd have to say that as my wife and I have tried over the years to increase our own faith and our family's faith, the greatest challenge we've faced is to really believe with all our hearts, to believe beforehand, to not doubt or fear, and to not give up. If you can do that and have an unshakable faith, you'll receive the blessings you seek—assuming, of course, that what you seek is in harmony with the will of the Lord.

I've heard some people say, "I'll try it, but I'm sure it won't work." And they're right. They're filled with doubt. And I've heard others say, "I don't know how this will work, but the Lord has promised, and I have confidence it will." And they're right, because they're filled with faith.

BELIEVE THAT NOTHING IS IMPOSSIBLE WITH THE LORD

When the Lord promised that Abraham and Sarah would have a child in their old age, and Sarah questioned it, the Lord responded, "Is any thing too hard for the Lord?" (Genesis 18:14.) And when the angel promised that Elisabeth would bear a son "in her old age," though she had always been barren, he said, "For with God nothing shall be impossible." (Luke 1:36–37.)

As we seek to receive answers to prayer, we must really believe that this principle is true. It seems the Lord does his best work in circumstances that are impossible— or near to it!

DO ALL THAT IS IN YOUR POWER; LET THE LORD DO THE REST

There is another way to express this principle: Pray as though everything depends on the Lord, then work as though everything depends on you.

If you will recall the experience we had in looking for the lost hat and wallet, we prayed repeatedly, then we got on the horses and looked. And we didn't just look for a moment, then quit. We looked as long as we could, praying in our hearts as we went.

When we obtain blessings from the Lord, it's not just because of the work we do. The work doesn't necessarily bring the blessing, but it does show our true desire, which enables the Lord to bless us.

Here is the principle, then: We must do all that is in our power, and then let the Lord do the rest. That suggests we need to find out what the Lord requires, then do it.

One thing I've learned over the years is that you need to count the cost up front. You need to clearly decide what you will do before you go after the blessing. What sacrifices and offerings does the Lord require? What are you willing to give? If you don't receive the blessing you seek, what are you going to do? Will you harden your heart? Will you become angry with the Lord? Will you say prayers don't work, or will you say, "Heavenly Father, I don't know why it didn't work. I gave it all I could and it still hasn't worked, but I know that it's not thy fault. Either it's not thy will or I have fallen short."

In my experience, the problem usually lies in ourselves. Often we have not sacrificed enough (i.e., paid the price) and thus the heavens cannot respond. But if you are willing to pay the price, the Lord will whisper to you and tell you some specific things you still need to do—a little here and a little there, then another month or two or three goes by and then you have it. Because you have offered what the Lord required, he can now respond. Of course, we must remember that all these principles are subject to the overriding will of the Lord. He will always do what is best for us.

DO WHAT THE LORD REQUIRES, BUT DON'T FEEL YOU MUST DO MORE

This is a corollary principle to the one we just discussed. We need to give the Lord all that he requires, but we do not need to give him more than he requires. Let me give you an example.

Some years ago I was living in Quito, Ecuador. I had to catch a flight to get to a stake conference in Caracas,

Venezuela. The number of problems I had with flights that day was unbelievable.

I was scheduled to fly on Ecuatoriana to Cali, Colombia, where I would connect with a flight to Caracas, but that flight was cancelled and I had to change flights and fly on Braniff. Unfortunately, Braniff failed to tell me that they had an hour stopover in Guayaquil, Ecuador. By the time I got to Cali, I had missed my connecting plane to Venezuela. I felt even worse when I saw the Ecuatoriana flight—the one that supposedly had been cancelled—there sitting on the runway in Cali. About that time I was getting really frustrated. I continued to try my best, with the help of the local mission president, to get to Caracas through Panama or by some other route, but I could not do it. After I'd missed my flight, airport officials told the two of us that they were having two days of national holidays in Colombia and that all the other flights out of Cali were booked. I was out of ideas and simply didn't know what to do.

At the mission home that night, I prayed to the Lord and said, "This is thy stake conference. I've done all that I know how to do to get there, and I have no more alternatives. What should I do now?"

That evening the mission president mentioned that a flight went from Bogotá to Caracas—if I could just get to Bogotá. He said the flight from Cali to Bogotá would take just half an hour. Unfortunately, we both knew that all flights were booked. The mission president then said, "If you really want to do all in your power, you could get on a bus right now and ride all night to Bogotá. Then you'd be there in the morning in time to catch the plane to Caracas."

I knew he was right. But I felt my evening would be

better spent if I stayed with the mission president and counseled and taught him rather than ride alone on the bus; and I also knew that the all-night bus trip would wear me out and make me tired and ineffective for the meetings of the stake conference. We prayed together and decided it would be best for me to spend the night in Cali; then in the morning I would try again to get a flight. I felt that the bus ride simply was not something the Lord required of me.

I knew there was risk with that decision. I might get stuck in Cali and miss the conference altogether. But I felt that that was the answer to my prayer: Wait until morning, then try again.

The next day there were still no seats, but the Lord opened the door and I got onto the flight to Caracas anyway—I was able to talk the pilot into letting me fly with him in the cockpit! I avoided the exhausting bus trip and had the whole evening to continue to work with that mission president.

When we're deciding how much the Lord requires, we need to be very careful. We want to do all he asks, but if we do more, we may be wasting time, energy, or money—and he may have other things he wants us to accomplish instead.

This principle of doing all we can, but not more than the Lord requires, relates to the truth that the Lord often exacts a spiritual price from us when we ask for blessings. Remember that the price you have to pay (the sacrifice) will vary from circumstance to circumstance. Sometimes you have to pay it straight out, while sometimes others will pay it for you, vicariously, or others will assist with their faith.

I believe that many people are confident that the Lord's will will be done and that the Lord can do anything, but they're not confident that he will do it for them or that he wants to do it now.

This lack of confidence in our ability to gain access to the powers of heaven is a major reason why more of our prayers aren't answered. In fact, as I travel around the Church I often meet people who say, "My prayer wasn't answered because it just wasn't the will of the Lord." They want to place the responsibility for their unanswered prayer on the Lord. But often the truth is that they just didn't exercise enough faith; they didn't have enough confidence in their ability to receive an answer.

It is true that we must ask according to the will of God. As John wrote:

> This is the confidence that we have in him, that, if we ask any thing according to his will, he heareth us:
> And if we know that he hear us, whatsoever we ask, we know that we have the petitions that we desired of him. (1 John 5:14–15.)

But too often we use this as an excuse. Instead of trying to place the responsibility on the Lord when we don't get the answers we want ("obviously it wasn't the will of God"), we should learn to have confidence before him so that we can "come boldly unto the throne of grace" (Hebrews 4:16) and receive the desires of our hearts.

How can we grow in confidence before the Lord? The scriptures provide some enlightenment that may help.

1. If we must ask according to the will of God, we can learn that will by revelation: "By the power of the Holy

Ghost ye may know the truth of all things." (Moroni 10:5.)

2. Confidence with the Father is possible because of the atonement of Jesus Christ, and comes to those who have faith in him: "I . . . preach among the Gentiles the unsearchable riches of Christ; . . . In whom we have boldness and access [unto the Father] with confidence by the faith of him." (Ephesians 3:8–12.)

3. Confidence comes to those who fear the Lord: "In the fear of the Lord is strong confidence." (Proverbs 14:26.)

4. Confidence before God comes as our hearts confirm that we are approved of him: "Let us not love in word, neither in tongue; but in deed and in truth. And hereby we know that we are of the truth, and shall assure our hearts before him. . . . Beloved, if our heart condemn us not, then have we confidence toward God." (1 John 3:18–21.)

5. Confidence comes as we receive the gift of charity and practice virtue: "Let thy bowels also be full of charity towards all men, and to the household of faith, and let virtue garnish thy thoughts unceasingly; then shall thy confidence wax strong in the presence of God." (D&C 121:45.)

If you feel that you lack confidence in your ability to receive answers from God, don't place the responsibility on him. You can choose to draw nearer to him, seeking to do those things I've just mentioned, and your confidence will grow.

Now here's a wonderful thing—you don't have to be perfect in these things to have confidence before God. You just have to be trying, honestly, as you go from day to day, and your confidence in him and in yourself will increasingly grow.

PRAY FOR WHAT'S RIGHT

We touched on this when we talked about growing in confidence. Our power in prayer grows when we know we're praying for those things that are in accordance with God's will for us.

Sometimes we pray for things with real intent that are not right for us. For example, before I went on my mission, I had a young lady whom I thought I really wanted to marry, and I was convinced that that was the right thing to do. I remember praying that the Lord would bless us that if it were right our relationship would prosper. But I was convinced it was right and felt there was almost no need to pray for it.

Then I got back from my mission and saw that she had her wedding dress and everything else ready, and it really scared me. That's when we truly got serious about seeking the Lord's will. The bottom line is that the marriage wasn't supposed to happen, and it didn't. She was a lovely young woman and continues to be a good friend of my family. But it wasn't right that I marry her, and how thankful we both are that the Lord provided us the mates we needed. How thankful I am the Lord didn't give me what I asked for.

BE HUMBLE, ACCEPTING
THE LORD'S WILL IN ALL THINGS

When you're dealing with the Lord, you simply have to have a humble heart. A prideful heart will very literally keep you from receiving answers. Part of humility is to be willing to subject yourself to the will of the Lord, whatever it is. If your heart is set right in the beginning, you can humbly say to the Lord, "According to my best understanding this is what I want, and I'm going to pray with all my heart to have it. But I know that I do not know all things (as thou, Father, dost), and if there is something I don't understand about this, I cheerfully submit my will to thine."

I think of a great example in the scriptures that teaches this principle. In Daniel 3, the king was preparing to throw three faithful Hebrew boys into the fiery furnace.

> Shadrach, Meshach, and Abed-nego, answered and said to the king, O Nebuchadnezzar, we are not careful to answer thee in this matter.
>
> If it be so, our God whom we serve is able to deliver us from the burning fiery furnace, and [then] he will deliver us out of thine hand, O king.
>
> But if not, be it known unto thee, O king, that we will not serve thy gods, nor worship the golden image which thou hast set up. (Daniel 3:16–18.)

My, what a great lesson is taught there. Those boys knew that God had power to deliver them, but they weren't positive that that was his will. Yet, in humility, they relied on the mercy of their Lord and trusted him to do what was best.

You remember in the story that the king then became so angry he heated the furnace up seven times hotter, so hot that the men who threw the Hebrew youths into the furnace died from the heat. Then Nebuchadnezzar looked into the furnace and said, "Did not we cast three men bound into the midst of the fire?" And his men answered, "True, O king." Then he said, "Lo, I see four men loose, walking in the midst of the fire, and they have no hurt; and the form of the fourth is like the Son of God." (Daniel 3:24–25.)

Jesus Christ, in his grace, intervened and saved these

boys because of their faith and their humility before God. They were willing to accept his will, and in this case his will was to protect, preserve, and save them.

BE FILLED WITH GRATITUDE FOR THE LORD'S BLESSINGS

To be filled with gratitude is one of the most important principles of receiving answers to prayer. As the Lord said in the Doctrine and Covenants, "Ye must give thanks unto God in the Spirit for whatsoever blessing ye are blessed with." (D&C 46:32.) Later he said, "He who receiveth all things with thankfulness shall be made glorious; and the things of this earth shall be added unto him, even an hundred fold, yea, more." (D&C 78:19.)

So what will happen if I'm grateful for what the Lord gives me? What did the passage say? I will receive more, "even an hundred fold."

In the story of the lost hat and wallet, we were blessed over and over again by this principle of gratitude. The family was grateful we had found the hat, even though we hadn't yet found the wallet. We thanked the Lord over and over again for the blessing of finding both missing objects. We even stopped the car after we left the ranch to offer another prayer of thanks.

My son particularly seemed to sense this truth. When he went into the bunkhouse after finding the hat, he knelt and prayed again. He said later, "I do not believe I would have heard the prompting to go over and stand by the coats had I not been offering a prayer of gratitude." I suspect the same thing happened for our missionary son as he rode his bike down that dark street in Mexico. Because he was pouring out his heart in thanks to the Lord, the channel between him and God was open and he was able to hear the warning voice that helped to save him from injury.

I don't believe it's possible to overdo gratitude with the Lord. He gives us so many blessings (most of which we're not even aware of) that I don't think we can ever thank him enough.

The Lord sets a wonderful example for us in being a great anonymous giver. You have to work at it to discover him doing good for you, yet he's doing it constantly.

Unfortunately, many men who lack faith say, "Well, God has never helped me. I've never been blessed in my life. Whatever I have, I've gotten on my own strength." It's my feeling they don't know what they're talking about, because the Lord blesses us constantly, as King Benjamin taught. (See Mosiah 2:19–25.)

Part of gratitude is to acknowledge the hand of the Lord in our lives. As the Lord said,

> In nothing doth man offend God, or against none is his wrath kindled, save those who confess not his hand in all things, and obey not his commandments. (D&C 59:21.)

I remember as a younger man I used to struggle with this issue of the Lord's hand in my life. "Was it really him or not? What if I tell him thanks and it wasn't even him?" I long since gave that up; I have become convinced that, just as the scriptures say, any good that ever comes to us comes because of the mercy and the love of the Lord Jesus Christ and his Father. I don't think it's possible to thank him for anything good that he has not been a party to.

The Lord has lamented that he cannot bless men if they do not acknowledge him as the giver of all good gifts:

For what doth it profit a man if a gift is bestowed upon him, and he receive not the gift? Behold, he rejoices not in that which is given unto him, neither rejoices in him who is the giver of the gift. (D&C 88:33.)

In other words, the Lord is saying, "What good is it for me to answer your prayers if you won't receive the answer, because you don't recognize the answer as having come from me?" When that occurs, we do not rejoice that we have received a gift, neither do we rejoice in the Lord, who gave the gift. The gift might as well not have been given. Conversely, if we recognize the hand of the Lord in our lives, asking for blessings and rejoicing in the receipt of every good gift, then the Lord will respond.

PRAY IN FAITH, BELIEVING YOU WILL RECEIVE

In chapter two we talked about having faith in Jesus Christ. In addition, we must believe that we will receive the thing we seek. For those seeking the Holy Ghost, the Lord has said, "ask the Father in my name, in faith believing that you shall receive, and you shall have the Holy Ghost, which manifesteth all things which are expedient unto the children of men." (D&C 18:18.)

The Lord further taught that "whatsoever ye shall ask the Father in my name, which is right, believing that ye shall receive, behold it shall be given unto you."(3 Nephi 18:20.)

Here is a great example of the Lord counseling us to believe and we will receive—yet, as always, the promise is conditioned on that "which is right," or the will of the Lord.

If you feel your faith is weak, you can pray as did the man who asked Jesus to cast a "dumb spirit" out of his son. And "Jesus said unto him, If thou canst believe, all things are possible to him that believeth. And straight-way the father of the child cried out, and said with tears, Lord, I believe; help thou mine unbelief." Then Jesus "rebuked the foul spirit" and healed the boy. (See Mark 9:14–29.)

Alma taught a great sermon about what to do if our belief is weak. He said:

> We will compare the word unto a seed. Now, if ye give place, that a seed may be planted in your heart, behold, if it be a true seed, or a good seed, if ye do not cast it out by your unbelief, that ye will resist the Spirit of the Lord, behold, it will begin to swell within your breasts; and when you feel these swelling motions, ye will begin to say within yourselves—It must needs be that this is a good seed, or that the word is good, for it beginneth to enlarge my soul; yea, it beginneth to enlighten my understanding, yea, it beginneth to be delicious to me. (Alma 32:28.)

We can grow in our ability to believe as we receive the Lord's word into our hearts, give place to it, and let the Spirit work within us.

UTILIZE THE FAST

"I give unto you a commandment that ye shall con-tinue in prayer and fasting from this time forth." (D&C 88:76.)

The story I just mentioned, in which Jesus cast the evil spirit out of the boy, also teaches us about the vital importance of fasting. Before Jesus came on the scene in that story, his disciples had tried, without success, to cast the spirit from the boy. After Jesus had done so, "his disciples asked him privately, Why could not we cast him out? And he said unto them, This kind can

come forth by nothing, but by prayer and fasting."
(Mark 9:28–29.)

Fasting is a small sacrifice we offer in an effort to
receive greater blessings from the Lord. When we fast in
an effort to receive an answer to prayer, we show the
Lord the depth of our desire, and, because we have exercised our agency in the sacrifice, we put ourselves in a
better position to receive the blessing we seek.

BE UNITED WITH OTHERS

To be unified in prayer brings more strength. If you
can get a number of people praying for you—a family,
your brothers and sisters, friends, ward members—the
unity in strength that results will help to bring increased
power to your request.

Over the years I've learned increasingly that when we
have a serious problem that is not too personal, we
should get all of our family to pray about it, especially
the little ones. They may not understand all the details of
what we need, but they can know enough to pray that
Dad or Mom needs this. And when they pray, they seem
to have a channel right into heaven. Not only can they
help you receive an answer to your prayer, but the very
process will teach them over and over again that the Lord
does answer prayer.

> As it is written—Whatsoever ye shall ask in faith,
> being united in prayer according to my command, ye
> shall receive. (D&C 29:6.)

PRAY FOR OTHERS

There is great power in praying for others, perhaps
even more than in just praying for yourself. The Lord

said to Thomas B. Marsh, who was then president of the Quorum of the Twelve:

> I know thy heart, and have heard thy prayers concerning thy brethren. Be not partial towards them in love above many others, but let thy love be for them as for thyself; and let thy love abound unto all men, and unto all who love my name.
>
> And pray for thy brethren of the Twelve. (D&C 112:11–12.)

When we pray for others with a fervent heart, we are obeying the second great commandment, to love our neighbors as ourselves. The Lord hears our pleas in their behalf and blesses them according to that which they are willing receive.

I've found it helpful to pray when I'm trying to help another, "Lord, deliver me his heart. How may I help this man now? How might I lighten his burden?" It's as important to pray specifically for others as it is for ourselves.

PRAY FOR AND WITH THE SPIRIT

The Spirit is the Lord's agent in bringing many blessings into our lives. The more the Holy Ghost can be with us, the more powerful our prayers will be.

"The Spirit shall be given unto you," the Lord said, "by the prayer of faith." (D&C 42:14.)

The Holy Ghost can even help us to know what to pray for. "He that asketh in the Spirit asketh according to the will of God; wherefore it is done even as he asketh." (D&C 46:30.) If we can receive the Spirit through a prayer of faith, we can then ask "in the Spirit," which will help us to ask "according to the will of God." Such prayers are always answered.

The Spirit can aid the process of communication in other ways:

> Likewise the Spirit also helpeth our infirmities: for we know not what we should pray for as we ought: but the Spirit itself maketh intercession for us with groanings which cannot be uttered.
>
> And he that searcheth the hearts knoweth what is the mind of the Spirit, because he maketh intercession for the saints according to the will of God. (Romans 8:26–27.)

It's evident that the Spirit will help us by revealing that for which we should pray.

LEARN TO RECOGNIZE THE PROMPTINGS OF THE SPIRIT

When you are attempting to obtain answers to your prayers and to be directed by the Lord, you need to learn to follow the promptings of the Spirit. Those promptings will help you know what the Lord requires of you as you seek the blessing. They will help you know what to pray for and where to go from there. The Spirit's promptings will also tell you as you go along how much more faith you may need to exercise in order to accomplish your desire. You may have promptings telling you what you need to repent of, how to draw closer to the Lord, specific steps toward the blessing, and so forth. In sum, the Lord will guide you through the experience if you will seek to follow the promptings he gives you.

You'll recall the story I told at the beginning of this chapter—how our missionary son was prompted to put both hands on his bicycle handles, and how that helped him avert a dangerous accident. That incident helped him to remember "how *quiet* the voice of the Spirit is. It is so quiet," he said, "that if you are not quiet you will not hear it." You may recall that he also said, "I believe if I had not been praying at that very moment, I would not have heard the voice. Because I was praying, I heard."

It is certainly true that when we are praying, we will hear the voice much more easily. As a rule, one must concentrate in order to hear the voice. It is generally felt more than it is heard. Because of that, if you are not calm and peaceful, you generally will not feel the words. Nephi said to his brothers:

> Ye have heard his voice from time to time; and he hath spoken unto you in a still small voice, but ye were past feeling, that ye could not feel his words. (1 Nephi 17:45.)

It truly is a still, small voice. As we read in Helaman:

> And it came to pass when they heard this voice, and beheld that it was not a voice of thunder, neither was it a voice of a great tumultuous noise, but behold, it was a still voice of perfect mildness, as if it had been a whisper, and it did pierce even to the very soul. (Helaman 5:30.)

Since the voice is so quiet, we have to really listen and expect to be able to hear it or we will not be able to. If we would like to increase our ability to hear the voice, it may best be accomplished by learning how to pray without ceasing. In my experience, the more we learn to pray throughout the day, the more the promptings will come and help us by inspiring us as to what to do.

I have seen the gift of recognizing promptings manifest many times in my wife, who often has a feeling or impression about something that is needed or lacking in one of our children. When we follow those promptings, they consistently lead us to additional experiences in faith; sometimes they've even saved a child from a life-threatening experience. Many other times they are more simple experiences where the child could have weathered things on his or her own, but because the Spirit of the Lord has been involved things turned out better than they otherwise would have.

In addition to the feelings we call promptings, the Spirit can also give us guidance, direction, and answers through enlightening our minds. The Lord said to Hyrum Smith,

> I will impart unto you of my Spirit, which shall enlighten your mind, which shall fill your soul with joy. (D&C 11:13.)

And to Oliver Cowdery he said,

> Thou knowest that thou hast inquired of me and I did enlighten thy mind; and now I tell thee these things that thou mayest know that thou hast been enlightened by the Spirit of truth. (D&C 6:15.)

If we will draw close to the Lord and learn to hear the voice of the Spirit, we will be able to receive the guidance and help we need, which will lead us to answers to our prayers.

Questions to Ponder

1. How can we establish an environment where we can hear the voice of the Lord?

_____

_____

_____

2. Why are we "commanded in all things to *ask* of God"?

_____

_____

_____

3. Why is it important that we be specific in our requests of the Lord?

_____

_____

_____

4. Why is it so important to cast out doubt and fear when we seek answers to prayer? (Ask yourself: How can I better cast doubt and fear out of my own mind and heart?)

_____

_____

_____

5. How can we find out what the Lord requires of us as we seek to receive his blessings?

_____

_____

_____

6. What are some specific suggestions given in this chapter about how we can increase our confidence before the Lord?

_____

_____

_____

7. Why is it vital that we accept the Lord's will in those things we seek? How can we learn that will and then bend ourselves to it?

_____

_____

_____

8. Why is gratitude so important in obtaining answers to prayers? (Ask yourself: How can I more fully show my gratitude to the Lord?)

_____

_____

_____

9. How can you increase your belief beforehand that the Lord will grant your request?

_____

_____

_____

10. In what ways can the Holy Ghost be a blessing to you in your prayers?

_____

_____

_____

11. This chapter contains a number of important principles that add power to your prayers. Which of these principles do you need to incorporate more fully into your life? How can you most effectively do it?

_____

_____

_____

CHAPTER 5

THE BLESSINGS OF PRAYER

A couple of years ago one of our sons fell in love with a hamster he called Hammy. This son has always loved animals, but he particularly loved Hammy. My son would let him crawl all over his back and up his shirt sleeve and into his shirt. He loved to walk around the house with Hammy in his shirt pocket. He had him sleep by his bed at night in a cage. He loved playing with him when he was doing anything and everything around the house. Hammy became my son's "favorite pal."

There were a number of times when Hammy got away from my son and he had to search to find him, but he was always able to do so.

But one day Hammy became lost and we couldn't find him. A full day passed with Hammy missing, and we were afraid he had become stuck somewhere or that he was lost and would die without food. My son had prayed about it and had searched with the whole family, but the hamster was nowhere to be found.

Our son told us he had done everything he could think of, and that nothing had worked. But then it dawned on him that although he had prayed, he had not *fervently* asked the Lord for help. He very humbly knelt in his bedroom and pled with the Lord to save his hamster and bring him back to him. The moment he opened his eyes he saw his hamster sitting on the rug next to him, watching him as if to say, "You, my friend, prayed me here."

What a small, yet powerful, example this was of how prayer can work. I bear testimony, as would my son, as to why the Lord did indeed answer his humble prayer. He prayed in faith, and he pled unto the Lord with a humble heart—and then he saw the Lord respond in a rather unique way.

It would have been one thing to have found the hamster some hours later, or even a few minutes later, but to have the hamster appear and be sitting on his haunches right next to my son as he prayed made the experience particularly impressive.

Some would say that the Lord has no interest in the small things in our lives. I use this example to show that the Lord cares even about a little boy and his hamster. And if that is true, how much he desires to bless us in big things!

THE KEY TO THE LORD'S BLESSINGS

The Lord truly wants to bless us in all aspects of our lives—our temporal needs, our goals, our relationships, our spiritual desires, and everything else. The key to receiving these blessings is to ask in prayer. Those who ask in faith and then obey the direction he gives them will receive the blessings. Of course, if we choose not to obey the Lord, we receive no promise, as a result of our disobedience.

I think many of us have a tendency to have our morning or evening prayers, and maybe even pray a few other times in a day, but not really pray. I'd ask you this question: When you face a new challenge in your day, what's the first thing that comes to your mind? Where does your heart run first? I hope it's to the Lord. That will be the case if you're trying to pray without ceasing. If you're not, I would say you're "winging it" on your own. You're trying to work through the day's many problems with the hope that your prayer in the morning covered it all.

It is most helpful when you move into any new circumstance, or when you are trying to assist others, that you have a prayer in your heart. "How should I deal with this? What should I do? Are there any special concerns that I ought to know about? Heavenly Father, help me. Help me."

Unfortunately, many of us don't ask. So we go off on our own and don't obtain the help we could have received with the problems we face each day.

Once again I bear humble witness that if we ask, as the scriptures say over and over again, we will receive. Again I bear witness that not one single, sincere prayer has been offered since the beginning of time that the Lord didn't respond to. Not one. Our problem is we don't ask. (Of course, the answer may come in a way we don't recognize or a way we don't like.)

If we will ask, we can have a much greater abundance of the gifts of the Spirit. Yes, we may need to increase our worthiness, but usually we're already worthy enough to obtain more, if we would only ask. Then those gifts will help us to grow in worthiness, that we can receive even more.

Please remember what we discussed before about being fanatical in these things. The devil is very good at working in the extremes—he succeeds when he motivates us to avoid prayer entirely, and he succeeds when he motivates us to spend hours on our knees when we ought to be out working on our problems.

Because the devil is not temperate or moderate, he will often be found working in the extremes. He's usually not able to get to religious, spiritual men and women through blatant sin, but he might be able to tempt them to excesses in the very gifts they have, perhaps even in the name of spirituality. Perhaps he will tempt them to fast and pray excessively. When we become excessive in these things, we might well open ourselves to receive direction from the adversary himself. Because of this, I feel a need to repeat my caution that you be careful and moderate in your efforts in things of the Spirit.

Perhaps the real key to all of this is the heart. Where is your heart? What is it you really desire? Do you really desire direction from the Lord? Are you willing to do your part to be sure you receive the proper answers to your prayers?

In this chapter I'm going to share with you a number of experiences (mine and others) that show the many kinds of answers and blessings the Lord is pleased to give us. Of course, these are only a small sampling. I hope you'll also remember the other examples included in this book. And if you were to record your own experiences, the number of examples could be increased many times over.

PRAYER FOR STRENGTH TO OVERCOME BAD HABITS

Some time ago I received a very special letter from a member who described how prayer was an important element in his effort to overcome a problem with alcohol and tobacco. Here's what he said (I've changed the names):

> I am writing to tell you of a very special blessing that has come into our home since Cindy entered the Missionary Training Center last October.

At the time Cindy went into the MTC, my wife and I both smoked and drank. We have been known to consume large quantities of alcoholic beverages. The Sunday after Cindy entered the MTC, I felt strongly compelled to quit smoking and drinking. It was Sunday night and we had consumed a great deal of alcohol that weekend. My wife's sister and her husband were visiting with us that night. I asked for help from anyone who could help. I didn't want to dishonor our beloved daughter's calling.

My wife's sister called a representative from Alcoholics Anonymous and talked to him. He offered to take me to their meetings and work with me if I wanted him to. I made arrangements to go to the next meeting.

My wife called our bishop, who came to our home, with his second counselor, that same night. The bishop suggested that we fast and pray for help with our smoking and drinking habits, then meet with him in his bishop's office for a special blessing.

I had been smoking for forty years and was a total alcoholic; my wife had been smoking for approximately twenty years and drank to keep me company. We fasted and prayed for twenty-four hours, then met with the bishop. He blessed us that we would be able to stop these habits and have no more desire for either alcohol or tobacco. The blessing was fulfilled immediately. When we left Bishop Stanley's office that night the desire for cigarettes and alcohol no longer existed.

I called the representative from Alcoholics Anonymous and told him I wouldn't need their help, since I had all the divine help I needed to conquer my habit.

I will be fifty-one years old in July, and now I know the power God has and the things that can be accomplished by him. I am sorry I waited so long to see the light. I have just been interviewed by our bishop to become an elder at our stake conference in June, and we hope to be married in the temple in August.

[This fine couple was indeed sealed in the temple that August, and their three children still living at home were sealed to them as well. One week after their missionary daughter returned from her mission, she also had the wonderful privilege of entering the temple and being sealed to her parents.]

It's valuable to review what helped this good brother and sister. Their daughter's missionary calling prepared their hearts, then prayer, fasting, and a priesthood blessing gave them the strength to follow through.

PRAYER FOR COMFORT
AND PEACE OF MIND IN TRIAL

When I was a mission president, a missionary once called the mission home about 2:00 A.M. saying his companion had left for the evening with a local companion and had never come home. My assistants drove to my home to inform me; when I got word, I immediately called the missionary and asked if there had been any problems the night before. He said no. I asked if his companion had been in a good mood before he left to proselyte that night. He said yes.

I thanked him, hung up the phone, and then knelt in my living room with my two assistants and offered prayer. As I prayed, I had the assurance that Elder Jones was all right and that we needn't worry. I didn't have any idea where he was or when he would return, but I knew he was okay. After we prayed, the assistants wanted to know what they should do next. I said, "I think you should go home and get some sleep. Remember, at 9:00 A.M. we're scheduled to travel to Paraguay." One of them asked me, "Do you mean we will go even if Elder Jones has not returned yet?" and I said, "No, he will be back. Just exercise faith and he will be back."

By 8:30 the next morning, Elder Jones still had not returned. The assistants and I were in the assistants' office. We prayed again and told the Lord that we had some very important things to do in Paraguay, and we wanted to know what to do. I felt the same thing I had felt the night before. "Don't worry about it; he will return before you leave." We stood from that prayer and I told my assistants, "Brethren, let's not worry about it. He'll be back in time."

About ten minutes before nine, when we had our bags packed and were ready to leave, Elder Jones arrived at the door of the mission home. Of course we were all relieved to see him. I immediately took him into the office to interview him about where he'd been and what he'd been doing the whole night. It turned out that in his great zealousness to preach the gospel, he and his local companion had gone to a neighboring town where no missionaries were assigned. He had gone into the home of a member family, had organized a group of people to teach, and had preached to them late into the night. It had not even crossed his mind that his companion would be worried about him. He had come in to the mission home, quite excited, to suggest that I open up a new city and place missionaries there.

I was so grateful that the Lord had answered my prayer. I bear testimony that the feeling of peace and assurance I had cannot come from men; it comes from the Lord. It enables you to go ahead with your task or your life with assurance—even though you're short on facts—that everything will work out all right.

PRAYER TO REMOVE
OBSTACLES TO RIGHTEOUS GOALS

Righteous goals are never easy. There are always obstacles. And it seems that as soon as we set a goal to really improve or to accomplish something worthwhile, not only do we face the expected obstacles, but we also begin to get all kinds of new opposition. The best answers to opposition and other obstacles are perseverance and prayer. Let me give you some examples.

As mission president, I had a set of missionaries who were having great success. How were they doing it? At one point, one of the missionaries answered that by bearing his testimony:

"I love my companion, and we are 100 percent in the work of the Lord," he said. "We have not approached one single door without either having a prayer in our hearts or having prayed in our car." And he said that they were thrilled to see doors, barriers, traditions of men, the things that blind people—all these obstacles just faded away.

Another missionary sent me this letter:

> I will never forget the beautiful experience we had of fulfilling a promise we made to a servant of the Lord, that of having ten baptisms in the month of March.
>
> It wasn't an easy task, due to the strong opposition of Satan. Up until the twenty-eighth of March we had only five baptisms, and we began to be quite concerned. For the whole month we had worked very hard and had tried to keep the mission rules 100 percent.
>
> On the twenty-ninth, my companion and I decided to fast so that nothing would go wrong with the baptism of a family of five we had scheduled that day.

However, that afternoon only four of them decided to
be baptized; that left us with only nine baptisms, and
in spite of all our efforts, we wouldn't meet our goal.
But the hand of the Lord manifested itself; while the
four were being baptized, the family member who had
decided against baptism approached us and said,
"Elders, I want to be baptized now."

I am so grateful to the Lord it is hard to express it.
My testimony concerning prayer and fasting has been
enormously strengthened, and the satisfaction I feel in
my heart for having kept a promise made to the Lord
is great.

I have seen in my own life how the Lord removes
obstacles to our righteous goals, particularly when we
approach him in earnest prayer. I had a wonderful experience with this principle once when I was trying to make
an important tour of one of our missions in Colombia. I
had arrived in Ecuador with my family on October 10,
with plans to go on to Colombia exactly one week later.
The day after we arrived we assigned some missionaries
to register our visas so they would be valid and so I
could use mine to travel to Colombia. The elders were
informed that it would take at least ten days to register
our visas—and we had only three working days before I
was to leave.

On Wednesday, October 12, I called the mission president and advised him to have an alternate plan in place,
since it looked like I probably wouldn't be able to join
him for the tour.

But we didn't just give up. We exercised our faith and
prayers, and we knew that the mission president and
missionaries in Colombia were doing the same. We con-
tacted the American embassy in Ecuador to see if I could
get a temporary travel permit, but it was not possible.

On Thursday, October 13, we visited the visa office to talk to the official who controlled the visas, to see if we could arrange some way for me to leave. When we reached the office he was out, but his boss offered to help us. We explained our problem. After listening to us for a few minutes, he confronted the person who had been causing our difficulty, asking if there was some reason why they could not register the visas. The man rather sheepishly said, "No, no reason. We can register them." The boss then suggested, "How about now?" So the man did it, and within the hour we had all seven visas registered and were out of the office.

I traveled to the mission in Cali, Colombia, on schedule.

I bear witness that the Lord is able to place his hand into difficult situations and turn them to our benefit—particularly when we ask him.

Let me give you one final example of how the Lord will remove obstacles to righteous goals if we will ask. Some time ago I was the General Authority visitor to a stake conference in a place quite far from the headquarters of the Church. The stake president approached me and said, "Elder Cook, as you know, this stake is quite new. The stake patriarch has been invited by the Church to go to Salt Lake City to conference in thirty days and, while there, to receive his endowments. He also wants his wife to go with him to be sealed, but he doesn't have any money. It will cost about $700. Does the Church have any funds to help so he can take his wife along?"

I had to tell him no, the Church doesn't provide funds for such purposes. He looked very discouraged and saddened. I then felt to add, "But President, if you will exercise your faith and have your patriarch and his wife do the same, he will go to conference and she will go with him. In fact, I promise you that if you will exercise your faith 100 percent, she will go. I promise you in the name of the Lord that the money will come forth and she will go."

As soon as I said that, the thought came into my mind, "Elder Cook, you are mighty free with my money. How come you are committing $700 of *my money?*" That was the gist of the message. In trying to respond to that impression, I quickly said to the stake president (who didn't know, of course, what was going on in my mind), "President, what I have told you is true. If by some chance you reach September 23 and you don't have the money, telephone me collect, because she is going." What I was really saying—without his knowing it—was that Elder and Sister Cook would pay the $700 if the Lord didn't. I didn't have $700 to spare. It would be difficult, but I would do it. It was as if the Lord said, "How much do you believe, Elder Cook?" And I responded, "I personally believe $700 worth that the money will be forthcoming." I suppose I didn't absolutely know what would happen. But I believed in my heart that she was going to conference.

Shortly before the thirty days had expired, a man came forward and offered to pay for the patriarch's wife to accompany him to Salt Lake City. To my knowledge, this good benefactor knew nothing of the president's request or of my promise. The Lord heard our prayers and touched this man's heart, and he responded.

The Lord desires that we be people who help make things happen. He doesn't want us to be thwarted by obstacles or opposition. He desires that we draw upon the all-powerful arm of God and add it to the power that resides in each of us. If we will do that, learning to do things in the Lord's own way, asking for help, the help will come.

PRAYER TO HELP HUMBLE A HEART

There is no greater miracle than a heart that is softened and humbled by the Spirit and then changed by the power of Christ. Prayer is a vital key in that process.

A few years ago a family named Jensen was baptized in New York state—except for one son. He seemed uninterested and continued with his worldly life. After some time one of the Jensen daughters began to attend Brigham Young University in Utah. She pestered her older, nonmember brother to attend, and he finally decided to try it. "Maybe there are a lot of cute girls there," he said.

He admits that upon his arrival at BYU his main thought was, "I sure hope they assign me a roommate who's a good drinking partner." Instead, he was assigned a faithful Latter-day Saint man, a young returned missionary who was paralyzed from the waist down and couldn't even walk.

As the weeks went by, Jensen came into the apartment night after night drunk, having been out with nonmember girls and having a good time. Finally his roommate, whom I'll call Smith, couldn't take it anymore. While lying in bed in the dark he said, "Jensen, you think you're pretty hot stuff, don't you?" he said.

"What do you mean?" said Jensen.

"You think you're really hot stuff. You can go out drinking every night, play around with the girls, and do whatever you want to do in this life, and you really think you're putting one over on BYU, the Lord, and everyone else. Well, I'm here to tell you that the Lord is going to call you to account, and you'd better repent or, frankly, you'll be going you know where."

Jensen shrugged it off. "I'm not so bad."

Smith wouldn't let it go. "What you need to do is repent. Tonight would be a good time to do it. You need to repent and put things straight with the Lord."

All of a sudden Jensen heard a thud. Smith had fallen to the floor. "Now he's praying for me," Jensen thought. He tried to ignore it. Finally he said, "Hurry up and finish your prayer and I'll help you back into bed."

Smith said, "I don't need to pray. I've already prayed. You're the man who needs to pray."

Jensen protested, but Smith wouldn't let up. Finally Jensen agreed and knelt alongside his roommate. It was the first prayer of his life, a simple prayer, but before it was over the Spirit touched Jensen, and he began to change at that very moment, even while he prayed. He agreed to immediately receive the missionary lessons.

Less than a month later he was baptized by his paralyzed roommate, with two other men helping to support him in the font. And a year later he was called on a mission. All as a result of one prayer offered in a students' apartment.

PRAYER TO HELP US TEACH THE TRUTH WITH COURAGE

When I was a freshman at Arizona State University, I was attending on a scholarship and was anxious to maintain a good grade-point average. Because of this, I signed up for a speech class that supposedly was quite easy. I felt it would enable me to earn the credits I needed, with good grades, without adding much to my workload.

After the last day had passed for being able to transfer out of the class, the teacher, a lady about sixty, said,

"Students, you will be pleased to know that in the last twenty-five years of my teaching, I've given only five A's." At those words my heart sank, and a general gloom settled over the whole class. I tried to transfer out of the class, but because the deadline had passed it proved to be impossible. I was disheartened, but as I thought about it, I wanted to rise to the challenge and make sure I received her sixth A. But as the months passed, even though I worked very hard on every assignment, I received B's, B-minuses, and once in a while a B-plus— but never an A.

Thirty days from the end of the term the teacher stood up and said to the class, "You each have one last speech to give. It will determine half of your grade. I want you to select a very controversial subject and give a twenty-five minute speech on it in front of the class. When you're finished, the class will try to tear apart your argument and your means of presenting it, while you try to defend it. Afterward, each student will provide a written critique of how you did."

A great hush came over the class, mostly from self-doubt and fear. Then they began to consider what they might talk about—communism versus democracy, racial issues, birth control, anything that might be controversial. I had no idea what topic I should address.

Numbers were drawn to determine who would speak first. I drew number nine. I remember the first three or four students who took their turns with that assignment. Some of the girls ended in tears. It was rough going—the class was quite critical. One Chinese boy was particularly sharp and was seemingly able to dismantle about anything we said. As the days went by and I saw how grueling the experience was, great fear mounted in my heart about what I should do.

I prayed about a topic but couldn't seem to settle on anything. The days passed—my speech was in two days and still I didn't have a topic. But one impression kept coming back to me: "If you're looking for a controversial subject, choose the Book of Mormon. You ought to defend the Book of Mormon in that speech class."

That idea made the speech even more frightening. Besides me, there wasn't a single member of the Church in the class. The teacher was a devout member of a Protestant church; she had even used the Bible in her teaching and had made it clear that as far as she was concerned, the Bible was the only revelation from God to man. I hadn't yet served my mission; I was a priest in the Aaronic Priesthood. But I had served a stake mission the summer before, and I knew the old missionary lesson about how the Lord, who is no respecter of persons, called prophets in the New World as well as the Old World.

I struggled within myself. I'd never been particularly frightened at speaking, but I remember that this time I really was. I offered many prayers to help me prepare and many more asking for help with the actual presentation. Still, when I stood to give my speech I had cold hands and a shaking feeling. I announced my subject as the Book of Mormon, then began teaching semihistorically and semiacademically, desiring not to offend.

But early on in the talk the Spirit of the Lord began to impress upon me the thought, "I can't just tell them about this book historically. I don't care what they think of me or what happens to my grade. The Book of Mormon is true. They ought to all know it."

I began to teach the lesson pretty much as it was written to be given to investigators, bearing my testimony frequently. As I did, a calmness came over me as the

Spirit began to bear witness to the twenty kids in the class that what I was saying was true. I spent the last three or four minutes answering the question, "How might a man really know if this book is true?" I read them Moroni's promise (see Moroni 10:4), and bore my testimony of its truthfulness. I said, "Say what you like, criticize what you want, but this book is true! And it came from God." I was so moved upon by the Spirit that I closed my talk "in the name of Jesus Christ, amen."

When I was finished there was such a stillness in the class that I wasn't sure if I was in real trouble or if the Spirit had truly enveloped the other students. I soon learned it was the Spirit. Finally the teacher broke the silence, trying to prompt and persuade them to attack, but they wouldn't. (I was pleased that one of the conditions she had laid down was that she herself, as teacher, couldn't participate.) When no one would comment, the teacher finally said, in frustration, "It looks like no one has anything to say. Be seated, Gene."

Later, as the students passed in their written evaluations, all their responses were positive. Four or five said, in essence, "Almost thou persuadest me." One girl said, "I am a Methodist, and I don't believe any of that about the Book of Mormon, but you almost convince me it is true." The Chinese boy who had been particularly critical said, "I've never heard of the Book of Mormon. Where could I get a copy?"

I know the Lord blessed me in that most difficult presentation. He does answer our prayers as we seek to teach others the truth. He blesses us as we keep the commandments and are not afraid to bear witness of him. As I went home that day these words from the Doctrine and Covenants came to me:

Therefore, verily I say unto you, lift up your voices unto this people; speak the thoughts that I shall put into your hearts, and you shall not be confounded before men;

For it shall be given you in the very hour, yea, in the very moment, what ye shall say.

But a commandment I give unto you, that ye shall declare whatsoever thing ye declare in my name, in solemnity of heart, in the spirit of meekness, in all things.

And I give unto you this promise, that inasmuch as ye do this the Holy Ghost shall be shed forth in bearing record unto all things whatsoever ye shall say. (D&C 100:5–8.)

I had surely seen the fulfillment of the promise mentioned.

Some weeks later I received a report card in the mail at my home. I opened it with some trepidation. How pleased I was to see an "A" written down for that speech class. My first thought was, "Truly she is a woman of integrity." I knew she didn't believe what I had taught about the Book of Mormon.

But then another thought came to me. "No, my son. I gave you that 'A.'"

What a wonderful preparation that experience was for a young man who found himself in the mission field some very few months later.

PRAYER AND A PRIESTHOOD BLESSING

Prayer can help us in many ways when it comes to priesthood blessings. It can help the priesthood brethren know what to say in the blessing so they can speak the will of the Lord. It can help the sick person and his or her family have a witness of the truth of what's been said. It can help them have a feeling of peace and comfort. And it can help everyone involved grow in faith.

I'd like to share with you an experience we had with my wife. She has a history of cancer in her family, so she was very concerned when she discovered a growth that appeared to be some kind of tumor. The doctor scheduled surgery to remove it, and we began to seek the Lord's blessings in prayer.

My wife was very concerned. Her worry was so great that she couldn't sleep well at night, and the anxiety seemed to follow her through her days. We talked about it, and she agreed that what she was really experiencing was doubt and fear.

The doctor planned to do a biopsy to see if the growth was malignant. As we talked, I realized she was waiting for the results of that test to see how she should exercise her faith. We discussed the fact that we could show greater faith by trusting in the Lord even before we knew if the growth was malignant. In other words, if we would pay the price of faith "up front," she could perhaps have the peace she needed from the Lord rather than relying totally on the doctor's test. She was very believing and determined to stop waiting to exercise her faith. I tried to exercise my faith for her, as did the children.

It surely seems to me that when one has a problem, if he will turn to the Lord and humble himself in the *first instance,* he is giving the greatest evidence of spirituality and faith. On the other hand, if we delay our reliance on the Lord, we may receive a lesser blessing.

At the same time as my wife began to exercise greater faith, I sought to prepare myself to give her a blessing. I fasted on one day and then again two days later. On that second day of fasting, which was to be the day of the blessing, I prayed as I drove to work, asking to know what I should say in the blessing. The Lord helped me to understand that he would reveal his will at the time of the blessing. On occasion we can know his will before we even go to give a blessing, but in this case I had the impression that the Lord wanted me to wait. I prayed intently all through the day that the Lord would be merciful in telling me his will as I blessed my sweet wife.

When I returned home from work that evening, I gathered the whole family together. I called on our ten-year-old son to offer a prayer. He, in his tender and tearful way, prayed that his mother would be all right. Afterwards, an older son anointed his mother, and then I sealed the anointing and gave the blessing.

I had prayed throughout the day that I would not say anything in the blessing except that which would come into my mind at the very moment. As I proceeded, I knew I should tell her that they would find that the growth was benign, that all would go well, and that at that time the next day she would be feeling fine, happy, and very much encouraged. We all felt the Spirit strongly.

We all slept well through the night. In the morning, when we went to the hospital, we both had a true feeling of peace.

The surgery lasted only an hour, the growth was benign, and she recovered quickly and completely.

Sometimes the Lord will allow a priesthood holder to be an instrument in healing someone. When that happens, prayer can enable him to come to a knowledge of the Lord's will, and it can help him to increase in faith.

In this experience, I don't know whether or not the Lord healed my wife, changing a malignant growth to one that was benign—and that's not really the point. What I do know is that, through prayer, the Lord blessed us with a knowledge of what to expect, and he granted us peace of mind.

One of the most important things I relearned in this experience is that the promptings of the Spirit are so subtle and so quiet that sometimes it is very, very difficult to know whether an answer is "yes" or "no." Sometimes it's very difficult to know whether you have been spoken to by the Spirit or not.

When the Spirit speaks, it is almost never in an audible voice that we hear with our ears. Instead, the Spirit usually speaks in feelings, thoughts, ideas, and impressions. The voice of the Spirit is still and small, and if we're looking for something more, or if we're not being very quiet and attentive, we'll likely miss the answer when it comes.

In this case, I had understood that the Lord would give me thoughts during the blessing, and I prayed in faith that whatever thoughts came into my mind at that time would be the Lord's thoughts. As I blessed my wife, then, I spoke what came into my mind, which was itself an exercise of faith.

The Lord gives this command and promise in the Doctrine and Covenants, which can be applied not only to speaking but also to giving blessings: "Speak the thoughts that I shall put into your hearts, . . .

"For it shall be given you in the very hour, yea, in the very moment, what ye shall say." (D&C 100:5–6.)

PRAYER FOR TEMPORAL ASSISTANCE

The Lord doesn't want us to be too deeply involved or absorbed by temporal, superficial, or secondary things. These things must be dealt with, but we must do it in a spiritual way.

I know of a man who was newly self-employed but was finding it impossible to get started. He had almost no money coming in—and a family to support. In addition, he had committed to contribute money to help build a new temple in his area, a commitment he fulfilled even though his finances were very shaky.

"I prayed very strongly this particular week," he said, "with much faith that the Lord would help us come up with some money so we could earn our way." Two hours after his prayer he received a phone call offering him his first work as a self-employed man. One hour later, another job came into his hands.

It is my testimony that the Lord will deliver those who pray in faith. He desires to bless us temporally, spiritually, and in every other area of our lives.

One morning a few years ago, I was reading in the Book of Mormon in 3 Nephi, chapters 13 and 14. As I read, I felt how foolish it is for any of us to feel that the Lord is not willing to help with our needs. (See 3 Nephi 14:7–11, which applies to temporal as well as spiritual blessings.)

The most impressive thought came when I was reading in chapter 13, where the Lord tells the Twelve that they ought not to be concerned about temporal things (food and clothing). Instead, he promises his servants that if they will exercise faith, he will clothe them, feed them, and take care of their temporal needs so they can continue in his service and do his will.

For some reason that thought settled very deeply in my heart. I was relieved to feel that even with all the temporal concerns I have, the Lord is willing to help me solve them if I will continue to concentrate on doing his work. And I need to add that I believe that promise is not just for General Authorities. I feel that he will bless any and all of us if our desire is to obey him and serve him.

That very evening my wife told me of a difficult plumbing problem we had in the house that we needed to resolve quickly. I dreaded trying to tackle such a problem, but I really couldn't afford to call a plumber. To make matters worse, I had to leave for a stake conference the next morning and needed to take care of the problem before I left. Unfortunately, after spending only a few moments on it I became absorbed in other matters and completely forgot about it until the next morning.

As I was getting dressed the next morning, I prayed two or three times that the Lord would solve the problem for me. I don't like doing those kinds of things very much anyway. As I prayed, the thought again came into my mind that if I would concentrate on preaching the gospel and saving souls, the Lord would help me with my temporal problems, including a plumbing problem. As I prayed, I felt reassured that he truly would help me.

It took some effort on my part—the problem didn't solve itself—but when the problem was resolved I knew with all my heart that it had been an answer to my prayers.

To some, such a blessing might seem like a small thing, but to me repair work is difficult and sometimes I don't feel very confident in it. I strongly believe that if something is a problem to you, whatever it is, it is a problem to the Lord, and he will help you. This experience gave me a witness once again that if we will truly seek to serve the Lord, he will help us with our temporal problems.

I'd like to share one final story that helps to illustrate this truth.

Some time ago the Church had a serious problem

with a local municipality in an overseas mission. The Church had had problems in this area for over a hundred years, and we needed a man and wife with great faith, as well as engineering expertise, to help us there.

We found a couple that fit the description. After they had been called and learned about the difficulties of their assignment, they were very much concerned about how they were going to resolve such a long-standing problem in just a year or two. We told them if they had faith the Lord would certainly help them accomplish it. I volunteered to give them a blessing to assist them in the difficult challenge before them.

A few days later we met for the blessing. This good man and his wife had a very humble spirit that day, and they indicated to me that even though they didn't know what they were going to do to solve the problem, they were totally confident.

"Why are you so confident?" I asked, and they said, "Because, we know the Lord will assist us."

Then this older man said, "Let me tell you a story.

"When I was a younger man, I was working for an engineering company in the United States. One day, when all of our technical experts were out of town on assignments, a company in Newfoundland called our engineering company asking for help. They had recently installed a huge, new industrial boiler, and it wasn't working. My boss didn't have anyone else to send and therefore said that he was going to send me. I was young and inexperienced and full of fear as he informed me of the assignment. I tried to talk my way out of it. He said, 'Well, you are the best we have. We have to send you.' And so it was that I traveled up to Newfoundland to try to help this company.

"As we walked around the plant, the plant managers

watched me check things out, then said, 'Well, what is wrong with this big boiler? Why won't it work?' I didn't know what to say, and I was filled with doubt and fear more than ever. Finally I answered, 'I need a few minutes to think about it.' I walked away, just leaving those men standing there, and wandered until I found a dark store-room. There I knelt in prayer and pleaded with the Lord that I would be inspired to know what to do. I told him that my boss and company were depending on me, as were these men in the plant. I said I had no idea what the real problem was and humbly asked the Lord to make it known to me. Then I closed my prayer and went back to where the men were waiting.

"We began again to walk around the big boiler. Finally one of the men said, 'Well, what is wrong?' The answer just seemed to come out of my mouth, and I said, 'There is no question about it; the boiler has been assembled backwards.' They said, 'What?' and I said, 'Yes, it has been assembled backwards. If you will call the plant that fabricated the boiler, they can tell you exactly what to do.'

"So they called the experts in the company that had originally constructed the boiler. They explained the problem and heard in response: 'Yes, it appears to us that the boiler has been assembled backwards. If you do such and such you will correct the problem.'"

After telling me this story, this faithful man, now retired, said, "Elder Cook, I know exactly what to do with this challenging assignment. I know that I must turn to the Lord, and then we will be able to solve this diffi-cult problem we face." I could tell by his faith, testi-mony, and determination that that is exactly what would happen.

As the next couple of years passed by, it proved to be

so. This good man and his wife truly worked a miracle in
the area in which they were called to serve.

Once again it is evident that faith in the Lord Jesus
Christ is sufficient to cover all our needs. The challenge
that most of us have is relying early enough, and fervently enough, upon that power which the Lord offers to
all of us.

OVERCOMING THE OBSTACLES TO PRAYER

As I've asked families and individuals around the
Church why they do not pray for such things as those
discussed in this chapter, I've been amazed at their
answers. Some are surprised that one would even think
to pray about these kinds of things. Others perhaps do
not desire to make the required effort. And still others
may feel that they lack the faith. Yet I know that the Lord
desires to help us in many things. When he offers a gift, it
pleases him most when we accept it.

When I've asked people why they don't pray more
consistently, I've heard a number of reasons:

—I don't have enough time.

—I just haven't gotten in the habit.

—My family just never did it, so I'm not in the praying mode.

—I believe I should. I guess I just haven't made a firm
decision yet to do it.

—I hate to admit it, but sometimes I don't believe that
prayer really makes that much difference.

Whatever your reason, I hope you'll remember that it
is the devil who teaches us not to pray. (See 2 Nephi
32:8–9.) I believe the devil has some of his most elite
emissaries trained in how to cause men not to pray. He
says simple things like, "You're too tired." "You can do it
tomorrow." "You can't take the time now—you have too

many other priorities." "Think of your sins—surely you don't think you're worthy to pray!" "Prayer doesn't work. Don't you remember the time you prayed and nothing happened?" Thus, on and on he goes in trying to convince people that prayer does not work, or is not worth the effort. Of course, all of these whisperings are lies.

I hope you'll make up your mind not to listen to the devil but to listen to the Lord, who consistently invites us to pray unto our Father in Heaven, that he may bless us.

In my judgment, all of our excuses and reasons for not praying can be resolved if we will just:

1. Decide that we ought to be praying,
2. Believe that it really will work, and
3. Decide when, where, and how we'll do it.

With respect to schedules, *if we're too busy to pray, we're just too busy.* We may have to get up a little earlier in the morning, or we may have to stay up a little later in the evening. We may have to adjust the time we are giving to a hobby or the time we spend watching television or going out for recreation. We may need to make an adjustment here or an adjustment there. But whatever we decide, we need to realize that choosing not to pray should not be an alternative.

If you are not in the habit, it is time to get in the habit. If you don't believe you should pray about little things, review the stories and testimonies of this chapter. If you don't believe prayer will work, it is time to put it to the test anew. I promise you that if you will follow the Lord and seek him with all your heart, he will surely bless you—and he will surely give you answers to your prayers.

Questions to Ponder

1. How can our hearts protect us from the excesses Satan would promote?

_____

_____

_____

2. In the experience of the alcoholic brother and his wife, what enabled them to overcome their habits?

_____

_____

_____

3. What are the best answers to opposition and other obstacles? How can you apply them in your own life?

_____

_____

_____

4. This chapter contains stories about how the Lord will help us in a number of important ways. How can you liken these stories unto yourself? (Ask yourself: How can I seek the Lord's blessings in more areas in my life?)

_____

_____

_____

5. There are a number of reasons people give for why they don't consistently pray. Are you guilty of giving any of these excuses? (Ask yourself: How can I repent and do better?)

_____

_____

_____

CHAPTER 6

PRAYER AS A BLESSING FOR PARENTS AND LEADERS

What parent hasn't prayed over a sick or wayward child? What leader hasn't spent time on his knees praying for those he's been called to serve and bless? Prayer is one of the most powerful tools we have as we seek to obtain the Lord's blessings in behalf of others.

Here are a few experiences that have solidified my testimony of the many ways we can use the power of prayer in our stewardships as parents in Zion and as leaders in the kingdom of God.

GUIDANCE IN DEALING WITH OTHERS

Once I had a very difficult interview with a man whom I'd known for a number of years. He had strayed from the teachings of the Church and had grown close to being excommunicated. Unfortunately, he wasn't being straight with his local leaders.

I struggled with him for about thirty minutes, trying to get him to open up to me—and to be willing to do the same with his stake president.

He was as hard as flint; he just wouldn't budge.

Finally, I could think of nothing more to say or do. I cried out to Heavenly Father for help, and as I prayed, the feeling came that I should go to him, put my arms around him, and tell him I love him. When I got up, he thought I was closing the interview. But instead I went over, took him in my arms, and told him I loved him with all my heart. When I did that, his heart melted and he yielded to the feelings of the Spirit. Finally he was willing to pour out all his troubles and all his sins—and, in the process, take the first steps to returning to worthiness and fellowship in the Church.

DISCERNING THE HEARTS OF OTHERS

Once when I was serving in a presidency, I learned I needed to replace one of my counselors. I discussed various possibilities with the local leaders and found myself leaning toward a Brother John Roberts (not his real name). I'd met him once and felt a good spirit about him.

When I discussed Brother Roberts with his stake president, however, he said, "He's never served real well. He was on a high council but didn't follow through and didn't always do what we asked him to do. He's now serving in a ward with the youth program."

I talked with leaders in the local area office of the Church, where he worked. They indicated some people had made some accusations against Brother Roberts in the past, suggesting that he had not been totally honest in his dealings with others. There was suspicion by these same people that some Church funds had been taken, but none of the allegations against him had ever been proven. I then learned that a General Authority who knew of the matter had come to Brother Roberts' defense, arguing that he was honest but hadn't been properly trained in accounting procedures.

I debated about it for some time. Should I call him or not? What was the truth about the allegations of dishonesty? As I prayed about it, I had a clear impression that he ought to be my counselor. I called my own General Authority adviser and discussed the matter at length with him. When I was finished, his counsel was, "If you feel good about him and the Spirit indicates he's the man, call him."

The Spirit had given that indication, and I obeyed. He'd been my counselor for less than a month when I recorded in my journal that he was capable of replacing me as the president. He had a great spirit, knew how to deal with other people, was faithful in his follow-through—he was everything I'd hoped for in a counselor.

It was a great delight later to see him called as a mission president.

The Lord knows his children much better than we do, and if we will go to him, in humility, he will help us to discern the hearts of those with whom we work. The lesson I learned from that experience was this: Follow the promptings of the Spirit, and all will be well.

Help in Reaching Others

Once when I was visiting the Chile Concepcion Mission, I met with most of the missionaries in a large meeting. As the meeting progressed, I found myself continuously praying on the stand concerning what I should talk about. I considered idea after idea and didn't feel good about anything I could think of.

Just before it was time for me to speak, all of a sudden two missionaries walked into the meeting at the back of the room—and they were trailing fourteen investigators behind them.

Since the meeting was to help us train missionaries,

the mission president and I agreed that the missionaries ought to take the investigators into another room to teach them. The president went back to tell them, but a few minutes later he came back and said, "Elder Cook, the missionaries ask forgiveness for bringing these investigators here, but they've promised them they would get to hear a General Authority. They've come a long distance to hear you speak."

We decided to allow them to stay for a little while so they could hear my testimony. When my turn came to speak, I still had no idea what the Lord wanted me to say. As I stood at the pulpit, however, I had an impression to invite all fourteen of them to sit on the front rows. I asked them a few questions and learned that they had all had three or four discussions, except one family, which had had only one.

I tried to prepare the spirit of my part of the meeting by bearing my testimony and talking about how it feels when the Holy Ghost bears witness of the truth. Then I said to the investigators, "I'd very much like you to help me teach these missionaries a lesson. Would you be willing?" They were quite surprised and didn't know quite what to say. But I forged ahead. "Will you visitors please tell us what it feels like to begin to get a testimony?" I asked.

One lady who was about fifty said, "I know it's true because I've read half the Book of Mormon. I have no doubt because I feel the Book of Mormon's true and I know that all the rest is as well." She bore a very powerful testimony, saying she felt true peace and tranquility in the teachings of the gospel.

A man then bore testimony that the Lord had helped him overcome some serious problems, and that he'd never felt better or more joyful than in the two weeks since the missionaries had been coming to his home.

I discerned that one woman was particularly weak in a testimony, and I had her come up to express her feelings. She said that she hadn't been very convinced about the gospel, but feeling the strength of the others had increased her own testimony. She decided she was ready to be baptized.

Then I invited a fifteen-year-old girl to come up and asked, "How is it that a fifteen-year-old girl can know these things are true?" She bore testimony that she'd felt the Spirit come into her heart and testify about Joseph Smith. She said that their home had had more peace and harmony and a more spiritual feeling since the missionaries came than at any time she could ever remember.

The investigators spoke of their love for the missionaries, and then I asked the two elders to come up and bear their testimonies and express their love to their investigators. It was very touching, and I understood that all fourteen expressed a desire to be baptized within the following couple of weeks.

In all, we spent nearly an hour with those investigators; then we let them go. There was little else I needed to do in the meeting. The missionaries had been taught, and they had received what the Lord had for them. Afterwards, I asked them what they had felt and made sure they observed the importance of the experience. All in all, it was a very spiritual experience.

I bear testimony that if we will humbly pray, the Lord will give to us, in the very moment, that which we should speak, and it will change people's hearts. I'm certain we accomplished more in those minutes with the investigators than anything I could have talked about on my own.

OVERCOMING WEAKNESSES
AND SOFTENING HEARTS

After a stake conference I attended in Colombia, I received a letter from a regional representative. He bore testimony of how prayer can help us touch the hearts of others—and strengthen us in our weaknesses at the same time.

> During the time we were together in the member conference in Cali, something very special happened to me that I want to share with you. . . .
> Among the teachings you left with the missionaries in the missionary session, you emphasized firmness, decision, the will and the wish to achieve something, and the spirit that we should have to fulfill our goal.

This regional representative mentioned that these were attitudes or character traits he had been struggling with. He didn't really have the will to be firm with those he directed in the work of the Church. He indicated that there were some serious problems in his region, but he just hadn't taken them in hand.

> I had prayed to the Lord, asking him to help me find a solution to this weakness in me. . . . That night, in the hotel, I asked the Lord to inspire me to know how to really receive help with this problem. Early Sunday morning, before leaving the hotel, I again asked in prayer for inspiration. . . . I know that the Lord always listens to me and answers me; that is why I had so much faith and was alert to hear his answer.
> It was for me a moment of decision when, ten minutes before beginning the general session, you told me, "José, it is very likely that Priesthood Leader So-and-so will not arrive at the conference. Some people say

that he will come, but I want to be sure. Please look after him."

I understood the magnitude of the challenge because I knew something of this priesthood leader's inactivity and resentment; but I also felt that it was of great importance to him and everyone else that he attend the session.

I set out with a young man on the journey, praying for the success of my assignment. Upon arriving at his house, I found him reading the newspaper with the television on. He was not dressed to go to church and, most sad of all, he had a very negative attitude. In a voice with which I had never heard myself speak before, but with strength and decision, I told him, "Brother, in the name of Jesus Christ and by special assignment given to me by Elder Cook, I came for you so that you can attend the conference."

His answer: "No way! With all the respect that you and Elder Cook deserve, I tell you that I will not go. Too many things have happened to me that . . . " I interrupted him to express our love and our hope that he would reconsider his attitude, but at the same time I showed firmness in my purpose: I told him I would not leave his house without him. I said that on another occasion we would talk about the problems, but for now we needed to get to the conference.

At that moment a marvelous change took place in me. Suddenly I understood that your sending me to that house had been a direct answer to my prayers. I had prayed for greater fortitude and spiritual strength, and the Lord had placed me in a circumstance where these could be tested and developed. I understood better than ever what it means to act in the name of Jesus Christ, by the power of the priesthood, and by assignment of a leader who is a servant of the Lord.

The minutes had passed and I thought that surely the conference had begun. But I said to myself, "I will not return to the chapel alone. If because of lack of strength I cannot get this priesthood leader to accompany me, I will stay here until the conference is over; then I will go home without going back to the chapel. But I will not leave here alone." I felt inspired by these words from Nephi: "As the Lord liveth, and as we live, we will not go down unto our father in the wilderness until we have accomplished the thing which the Lord hath commanded us." (1 Nephi 3:15.)

Somehow this good man must have felt that decision, because even though he expressed thousands of reasons for not going, after we knelt in prayer he felt some remorse for having made me miss part of the conference. He said: "Oh, all right! I will go, but only with the condition that as soon as the conference is over I will return to my house."

I accepted with great joy, asking the Lord to help this priesthood leader to find so much love and understanding in the chapel that he would be willing to change his attitude.

Never have I seen a man get ready in as little time as he did. In five minutes he was ready to accompany me, and he looked the part of a leader, touched by the Spirit, ready to attend to his duties.

STRENGTHENING OUR BRETHREN

I know of a stake that advanced some 150 men to the Melchizedek Priesthood within a very short period of time. What did the ward and stake leaders do? What enabled them to awaken so many men who had been spiritually slumbering?

As we interviewed the leaders of this stake, we discovered that their success began with a spirit of resolve. As one bishop said: "As far as I'm concerned, the day it began was when the stake president *decided* that is what we would do. I don't mean he just thought it would be a good idea or that he would try. *I mean he decided.*"

This stake president decided that he could no longer tolerate in his stake the kind of action that would allow increasing numbers of men to end up in the pool of prospective elders.

The Lord taught this principle, the spirit of resolve, through Nephi when he said, as we have just quoted,

> As the Lord liveth, and as we live, we will not go down unto our father in the wilderness until we have accomplished the thing which the Lord hath commanded us. (1 Nephi 3:15.)

Once they'd made the decision, the leaders became totally reliant on the Lord. They humbled themselves. They sincerely and intently *asked* the Lord for help. One bishop said: "Once we sensed the spirit of the stake president, that he really meant it, we realized that we had never done anything like that before. We went to the Lord and fasted together and prayed, 'How will we do it? What shall we do?'"

As they sought to move forward with their desire, they continued to seek the inspiration of the Spirit. Another bishop said: "I didn't just focus on the six easy steps of interviewing I'd been taught. Instead, I decided the Lord would have to tell me what I had to do to help each man come to a change of heart. Some men I interviewed alone, as the bishop; others I interviewed with the stake president or my elders quorum president. In each instance we prayed without ceasing, pleading that the Lord would deliver up each man's heart to us."

The Lord has promised that he will use us as instruments in his hands to assist in the conversion of his people.

And if thou wilt *inquire,* thou shalt know mysteries which are great and marvelous . . . that thou mayest bring *many* to the knowledge of the truth, yea, convince them of the error of their ways. (D&C 6:11; italics added.)

Part of their plan was to interview every prospective elder in their stewardship. One bishop said, "With every man who came in, we knelt in prayer and I pleaded with the Lord in the presence of the man that he would feel the Spirit and desire to be reunited to full fellowship with the Lord and his Church. Most of these men were not easy ones. Most were long-term inactives, not new converts."

Another bishop said: "I literally interviewed every man, woman, and youth in my ward. I quit just talking about it and interviewed with the Spirit. I challenged whole families to come and be a part of the kingdom. We specifically challenged the husband and wife to attend a temple preparation seminar, which was set for a specific date. We told them the Lord expected them to be there, and that he had sent us to deliver that message to them. What a thrill it was to see them respond. Our brethren, the prospective elders, literally felt the love we extended to them. They could not do anything but respond. The love was constant and strong and very overpowering because it wasn't just us but the Spirit of the Lord in us."

The success in this stake came from three simple spiritual elements. First, the leaders had the spirit of resolve: "We will do it." Second, they centered their minds totally on the Lord, knowing that he is the one who delivers up the hearts of the people; and they specifically asked him for that blessing. Third, in the spirit of prayer, they worked hard, interviewing everybody by the Spirit to cause them to repent, feel loved, and return to the fold.

Touching and Changing Hearts

Another stake had a similar experience. At a stake conference I was amazed at the number of worthy young men who had not been on a mission, even though they were of age. There were so many at the conference that I had them stand up. Seventy-six of them stood. I was overwhelmed. And I wondered in my heart, where are our leaders?

After the conference I called a special meeting of the stake presidency and bishops. When we were finished I left them with a challenge: "Brethren, I'd like to ask you to interview every one of those young men, all seventy-six of them. Talk to them in the Spirit of the Lord and invite them to respond to his call. Please get back to me in a couple of months and give me a report on each one."

About six weeks later, the stake president came to me with a report. He said, "Elder Cook, we've completed every one of the interviews."

"That's great," I responded. "How many are going on missions?"

He paused. He was pleased that all the young people had been interviewed, but he didn't want to tell me how the interviews had turned out. Finally he said, "Well, there are three or four. And there are five or six others who will probably go next year."

I prayed. What should I say? Then I felt that the Lord wanted me to speak boldly, and I said, "President, I can come to only one of two conclusions."

"What's that?" he asked.

I said, "It may be that this is the most unworthy, unresponsive group of young people I've ever met."

He shook his head. "No, that's not right, Elder Cook. These are great young people."

"I know they are. I visited with a number of them at the conference."

We talked about the youth for a few moments, and then he said, "What's the other conclusion?"

I said, "I guess this one has to be true then, if the other one was false."

"And what is that?"

I would never have answered him if the Lord hadn't directed me to, but I could tell it was important that I be very forthright. I said, "I guess I've found the most ineffective group of priesthood leaders I've ever met." And I didn't crack a smile.

The stake president took it hard, and I knew he would. But the bottom line was that he needed it. He was not acting as humbly as he should have. He had gone out and operated like a man, and that's why he got the results he did.

As we concluded the interview, I put my arms around him and I loved him. We knelt and prayed together. Then I bore my witness to him: "President, you go out now and act in the authority of God, and he will respond. You go into the homes of those young men and kneel down and pray with them. You ask each one to explain to the Lord in your presence why he can't go on a mission. Then if the Lord says he doesn't have to go, it's okay with me. But if the Lord says he has to, then tell the boy to be honorable enough and get on with it." We agreed we'd meet in another six weeks and he would give me another report.

After the meeting I called his regional representative and said, "I just had this difficult meeting with President So-and-so. I'm sure he's feeling pretty low. Will you go to him and strengthen and bless him?"

Six weeks later this stake president came back with his report. Here's what he said:

"Brother Cook, I went out of your office terribly offended. I was humiliated and angry. I stewed for a whole week. During that whole time, I was absolutely miserable.

"Finally I mentioned it to my wife. She heard me out, and then said, 'My dear, I don't want to offend you either, but a servant of the Lord talked to you and I feel a burning in me that tells me he spoke for the Lord. He's only asking you to go and talk to them again. Quit fighting it. Do it.'

"I knew she was right. For the first time I humbled myself and desired to do it the Lord's way. We knelt and prayed together, and a great power came over me. I felt I could do anything, even move a mountain, and I said, 'I will go and do it without further excuse.'"

So he went out and, with the help of his bishops, began to interview these young men again. After six weeks he had interviewed twenty-seven men. Twenty-five of them had agreed to go on missions and were filling out their papers. Prayer had softened his heart and enabled him to go forth, and prayer softened the hearts of the young men, that they would respond.

Two examples will illustrate his experiences.

One young man who often visited the stake president's son was on the list of those to be interviewed. I'll call him John. He was only partially active and had no desire to go on a mission, but he was basically worthy and should have been preparing to go.

One day John came to visit the stake president's son. When the president saw him, he immediately started praying, "Heavenly Father, what should I do? What should I say to this young man? How can I touch his heart?" Then the president said out of the blue, "John, I hear you're going on a mission."

John was surprised. "President, you know I have no intention of going on a mission. Who told you that?"

Then the president, in great sincerity, said by the Spirit, "The Lord, my boy, and the Holy Ghost." John didn't know what to say. Then this good stake president said, "John, let's pray." They knelt down right then and prayed, and in a matter of four or five minutes, John decided he was going on a mission. What changed him? The Spirit of the Holy Ghost, which came to him strongly as he and the stake president prayed.

But that's not the end of the story. John was worried that his parents, who were inactive in the Church, would not support him on a mission. The president said, "Don't worry about that, John. If the Lord wants you to go, we're not worried about anybody else, are we?"

"Well, I guess not."

They visited his parents and prayed with them. In less than twenty minutes the parents agreed, and John had the opportunity to serve a mission with his parents' support.

This same stake president had another experience that illustrates how powerful prayer can be in helping us touch the hearts of others. One of his members was a young lady, twenty-two years old, who wanted to serve a mission but whose nonmember parents objected. They had two concerns: that their daughter would lose her chastity in the mission field and that she would lose her current job in a country where unemployment was very high.

The stake president visited them in their home and offered a constant prayer in his heart for help from the Lord. He didn't know what to do or say, but he had faith the Lord could help him. As they talked, he suddenly thought of a young returned-missionary sister who lived nearby. He excused himself and went to get her, praying all the way that she would be home and available. She was home, and she willingly agreed to bear testimony to these nonmembers. She told them more about what a mission was, how it had changed her life, and how it had strengthened rather than weakened her moral values.

The parents were pleased and convinced—but still were concerned about their daughter's employment. The stake president next visited the girl's boss, the manager of a department store and explained what the young woman was trying to accomplish. The manager was unimpressed. The young woman was one of his best employees, he said, and he wasn't about to let her leave for eighteen months. If she did choose to leave, she'd lose her job.

Continuing to offer a silent prayer, the stake president explained how beneficial the mission would be. The manager's heart was touched, and he offered to sign an agreement to allow her to return to her job after her mission—which was unheard of in that country at that time. He also offered to help support her on the mission, giving a sum of money on the spot.

I bear my testimony that if we will ask, the Lord will help us in our conversations, our visiting, our interviews, and all our contacts with those whom we serve.

We must pray fervently throughout all such contacts that we may "speak the thoughts that [the Lord] shall put into [our] hearts, and [we] shall not be confounded before men; for it shall be given [us] . . . in the very moment, what [we] shall say." He surely will give us "that portion that shall be meted unto every man." (D&C 100:5–6; 84:85.)

Truly prayer will help to change our hearts, and it will help to touch the hearts of those with whom we work. Whether we're dealing with a rebellious child, an unhappy spouse, a less active member, a friend or associate, or even ourselves, prayer can make a real and lasting difference.

Questions to Ponder

1. Review the letter from the regional representative. How did prayer help him with the problem with the priesthood leader?

_____

_____

_____

2. How did prayer make a difference in the story of the stake that advanced 150 men to the Melchizedek Priesthood?

_____

_____

_____

3. How did prayer make a difference in the story of the stake president who interviewed seventy-six young men for missions?

_____

_____

_____

4. Prayer can be a great power in helping to change people's hearts. How can you use prayer to help family members whose hearts need to be changed? How about those with whom you work in the Church or at your place of employment?

_____

_____

_____

5. This chapter has a number of stories about how prayer can help parents and leaders. How can you use prayer as a blessing to help you with your struggles as a parent or in your Church calling?

_____

_____

_____

CHAPTER 7

THE GRACE OF THE LORD

How many of us sometimes try to resolve life's challenges ourselves, without seeking the intervention of the Lord in our lives? We try to carry the burden alone.

How many times, likewise, as we have prayed for assistance or help with our problems, have we severed ourselves from the power of God because of doubt or fear and thus could not obtain the blessings he would give us? (See D&C 6:36; 67:3.)

As some are faced with trials and afflictions, they say, "Why won't God help me?" Some have even struggled with doubts about their prayers and their personal worthiness and say, "Perhaps prayer doesn't work."

I bear testimony that prayer does work, and that the Lord stands ready to help us. One of the keys seems to be to learn better from the Lord how to engage the powers of heaven to intervene in our behalf, which we do when we receive his grace.

THE ENABLING POWER OF GOD

The best definition I know of the word *grace* is found in the dictionary of the LDS edition of the Bible. It says:

> The main idea of the word is divine means of help or strength, given through the bounteous mercy and

love of Jesus Christ. . . . Grace is an enabling power.
(*Holy Bible* [Salt Lake City: The Church of Jesus Christ
of Latter-day Saints, 1979], Appendix, p. 697.)

Grace, then, is the enabling power of God. In fact, we
could replace the word "grace" with "God's divine
enabling power" every time we see it in the scriptures,
and we'd have a great insight.

Let me give you an example from Jacob:

Wherefore, we search the prophets, and we have
many revelations and the spirit of prophecy; and having all these witnesses we obtain a hope, and our faith
becometh unshaken, insomuch that we truly can command in the name of Jesus and the very trees obey us,
or the mountains, or the waves of the sea. (Jacob 4:6.)

What a great statement! The mountains and trees and
waves of the sea responded to their command. But how
were they able to do that?

Nevertheless, the Lord God sheweth us our weakness that we may know that it is by his grace [or his
enabling power], and his great condescensions unto
the children of men, that we have power to do these
things. (Jacob 4:7.)

How is it you have power to do it, Jacob? It was
because of the grace, the enabling power of God, and his
condescension unto the children of men.

Let's look at another scripture that underscores how
important this enabling power is:

There is a law, irrevocably decreed in heaven before
the foundations of this world, upon which all blessings
are predicated—
And when we obtain any blessing from God, it is by

obedience to that law upon which it is predicated.
(D&C 130:20–21.)

This is one of those all-inclusive revelations. The law
was *irrevocably* decreed—it cannot be changed. *All* blessings are predicated upon that law—none are excluded.
When we receive *any* blessing, it is by obedience to the
law—again, none are excluded.

I believe the Lord is saying that there are laws and
conditions that govern all blessings. If you fulfill the law
and the condition, the blessing will be yours (assuming
you're not working contrary to the will of God).

How does this fit into the principle of grace?

Let's assume that a faithful man named John is praying for a blessing with all his heart, and he does all he can
to help bring it to pass, but it's just not enough. He puts
in most of what's required but not all. He just doesn't
have the capacity to do all that's required. But he persists
and receives the blessing.

Question: Who put in the rest? The law or requirement must be fulfilled, but John wasn't able to fully do it.
Who compensates for his inadequacy?

Answer: The Lord, Jesus Christ. The enabling power
of God, or grace, intervened and Jesus Christ contributed
what John lacked. And thus the law was fulfilled.

Please understand this. Jesus came not only to save
us from our sins but also to assist us with our infirmities,
our afflictions, our weaknesses, our problems, and our
discouragements. And when he does so, in the process he
helps us to qualify for the blessings we seek, and that is
called grace.

Now consider another man. This man has less faith
than John. This man was baptized just last week. He
seeks the same blessing as John, but he cannot muster the

faith that John has. As he seeks to obey the required law, all he can do is put in maybe a tenth of what's needed. Yet he still receives the blessing. Why is that? Again, because Jesus compensated and put the rest in for him. After we have done all in our power, the grace of the Lord will intervene. The prophet Nephi said it masterfully:

> For we labor diligently to write, to persuade our children, and also our brethren, to believe in Christ, and to be reconciled to God; for we know that it is by grace that we are saved, after all we can do. (2 Nephi 25:23.)

In my judgment, this principle explains why it is that when a little child prays he can so readily receive the blessing. The child doesn't know how to do very much except give all of his heart, but that's enough. Then the Lord puts in the rest. Children have great access to the heavens.

We also can have such access if we will pray with all our hearts and do all we can to qualify for the blessing we seek. Then, through the grace, or enabling power, of Christ, the heavens will intervene and bring us that which we desire.

But I want to stress once again that all of these principles are always subject to the overriding will of the Lord. Because of his great love for us, he will always do what is best for us in the short term as well as in the long run.

ACCESSING THE LORD'S GRACE

Since these things are true, how can you obtain access to this grace that we're talking about, so the heavens can help you? How do you fulfill the laws and the conditions for grace? The scriptures teach of some prerequisites.

First, have faith. As Paul wrote:

> Therefore being justified by faith, we have peace with God through our Lord Jesus Christ:
> By whom also we have access by faith into this grace. (Romans 5:1–2.)

If we truly have faith, casting out doubts and fears, we can receive grace, which can give us power unto the answering of our prayers.

Second, repent and do good works. As we read in Helaman:

> Therefore, blessed are they who will repent. . . .
> And may God grant, in his great fulness, that men might be brought unto repentance and good works, that they might be restored unto grace for grace, according to their works. (Helaman 12:23–24.)

A repentant heart and good works are the very conditions required to have grace given to us. When someone pleads fervently in prayer for a blessing, the answer may be conditioned on repentance from our own personal sins more than any other factor. (See D&C 101:7–8; Mosiah 11:23–24.)

Third, be humble. James said:

> He giveth more grace. Wherefore he saith, God resisteth the proud, but giveth grace unto the humble. (James 4:6.)

Humility seems to rest at the core of who we are in our hearts. If you'll humble yourself before God—and if your desire is in harmony with the will of the Lord—the grace will come, the power will come and intervene for you, and your prayer will be answered.

This principle was also given by the Lord through Moroni:

> And if men come unto me I will show unto them their weakness. I give unto men weakness that they may be humble; and my grace is sufficient for all men that humble themselves before me; for if they humble themselves before me, and have faith in me, then will I make weak things become strong unto them. (Ether 12:27.)

If we will come unto Christ, have faith in him, and humble ourselves before him, then he will give us the grace. How much grace? As much as we need—his grace is sufficient for all men.

Fourth, do all in your power. Nephi gave us this great statement of truth:

> We know that it is by grace that we are saved, after all we can do. (2 Nephi 25:23.)

In other words, you can't get the grace, or enabling power, to work for you unless you have done all you can do. When you've done all you're able to do of what the Lord requires, you have every right to expect the Lord to intervene, and he will, assuming you're seeking something that's honorable and right.

This truth was reaffirmed in an inspired way by Joseph Smith when he said,

> Let us cheerfully do all things that lie in our power; and then may we stand still, with the utmost assurance, to see the salvation of God, and for his arm to be revealed. (D&C 123:17.)

Unless one has done all in his own power, he cannot expect the grace of God to be manifest. What a glorious principle to understand: the Lord's assistance to us—whether we have strong faith or weak faith; whether a man, a woman, or a child—is not based just on what we know, how strong we are, or who we are, but more on our *giving all that we can give* and *doing all that we can do,* according to the Lord's requirement and according to our present capacity. Once we have given all we can, then the Lord, through his grace, may assist us.

Fifth, keep the commandments. This requirement is very closely related to the one of repenting and doing good works. The Lord has said,

> If you keep my commandments you shall receive of his fulness . . . ; therefore, I say unto you, you shall receive grace for grace. (D&C 93:20.)

To obtain grace, one does not have to be perfect, but he does have to be trying to keep the commandments the best he can. Then the Lord may allow him to receive that power.

These, then, are some key elements that are needed as we seek to receive grace, which in turn will bring us blessings and strength from above: faith, repentance and good works, humility, doing all that is in our power, and keeping the commandments.

I bear witness that if we will seek the grace of God, he will come to our aid and the aid of our loved ones in times of need. He will hear our pleas and, according to his holy will, he will give us answers to our prayers. He will intervene in our behalf and will give us the blessings we seek. If we do our part, then surely he will do his.

Let us therefore come boldly unto the throne of
grace, that we may obtain mercy, and find grace to help
in time of need. (Hebrews 4:16.)

Questions to Ponder

1. What is the meaning of the word *grace?*

_____

_____

_____

2. If we seek a blessing with all our hearts, and it is the will of
God, but we don't have the capacity to do all that's required,
what will the Lord do to help us?

_____

_____

_____

3. What are some of the prerequisites to receiving grace?

_____

_____

_____

4. The Lord's assistance to us is not based so much on what we
know, how strong we are, or who we are, but more on our giving all we can give and doing all we can do. When you're
struggling to receive an answer or a blessing, ask yourself what
more you can give. What more can you do to receive the Lord's
blessings?

_____

_____

_____

5. We don't have to be perfect to receive grace. But what must we be doing in order to receive this gift from God?

_____

_____

_____

CHAPTER 8

WHEN ANSWERS
DO NOT SEEM TO COME

Not long ago I received a poignant letter from a single sister in the Church who had had a disappointing experience with prayer. As she had prayed about a man she was interested in, she thought she had been inspired to know she would marry him, but in her view it never worked out. Here is part of her letter:

> Last year I met a man (I'll call him Paul) who quite impressed me with his compassion and his other qualities. I became attracted to him—which was a rare event for me, since I'm forty-eight years old and have never been married. As my feelings for him started to grow, I began a process of prayer to know if I should expect the relationship to develop. I prayed very carefully, because I didn't want to pray for something that was wrong—and I didn't want to pursue something that would only end in my being hurt. From my first carefully worded prayer, I felt as if it was part of an eternal plan for us to be together.
>
> I've prayed about this every day for many months. I've fasted many times; I've gone to the temple and prayed in the celestial room. Every time, I've received the same intense feeling within that I experience when the Spirit bears testimony to me about the truthfulness

of the gospel. Sometimes when I've had this intense feeling, I've explained to my Heavenly Father that I interpreted the feeling as a confirmation about Paul and me, and I've asked Him to take the feeling away if I was misinterpreting its meaning. That never happened.

However, it has now become painfully clear to me that there will never be a relationship between Paul and me. This is most confusing, as well as anguishing. Of course there is the emotional pain—I've prayed about marriage for many years. (I was engaged in 1984, but my fiance abruptly decided to marry another after his prayers about our marriage suddenly felt "wrong.") But the greatest pain is spiritual. I honestly feel forsaken by our Heavenly Father. How could something that feels so spiritually right, as a result of sincere and fervent prayer, turn out to be so wrong?

Of course, the standard explanations are: (*a*) I confused my emotional feelings with spiritual answers; or, (*b*) Paul chose not to be guided by the Spirit.

My responses to these standard explanations are: (*a*) Not only are the intense feelings that I experienced during my prayers the same as what I feel about other spiritual matters, but I also can't force them to occur; and (*b*) if Paul chose not to be guided by the Spirit, God would have known that in advance, and He could have spared me this painful ordeal just by letting me know it would not work out.

It is incomprehensible to me that my earnest actions have not brought blessings but have left me in the depths of despair. Can't we expect to receive divine guidance if we live righteously, pray sincerely and fervently, fast, listen to the Spirit, and ask for confirmation of the answers we receive? Despite some very painful experiences at other times in my life, this is the most depressing experience I've ever had, because I truly feel betrayed by God. I would much rather have a

terminal illness than face the rest of my life not knowing what to believe when I pray.

DEALING WITH UNANSWERED PRAYERS

As I meet with members of the Church in many
lands, it is abundantly clear that this sister is not alone in
her frustrations with answers to prayer. All of us struggle
to some degree with how to receive answers to our
prayers. We all have times when answers come easily. We
have times when answers come clearly and distinctly.
And we all have times when we really pray about something and seemingly receive no answer. On some such
occasions, we may feel that we've conscientiously followed the instructions in Doctrine and Covenants 9:7–9.
We have studied the issue out in our minds, prayed
about it (perhaps we even fasted), and asked the Lord if
our decision or understanding is right. But after all that,
we still do not feel we have received a burning in the
bosom—or a stupor of thought—and thus it appears we
are left to our own resources to try to solve the problem.
Or we may be certain we have received an answer—but
then things don't work out the way we thought they
would.

When these kinds of situations arise, it presents an
even greater spiritual opportunity to exercise our faith
and to persist—and thus, in the process, to truly increase
our faith, perhaps more than when answers come easily,
directly, clearly, or distinctly.

Some Saints, when they have faced situations like
this, lose faith in prayer, or determine the Lord doesn't
always answer prayer, or decide it is not a surefire means
of receiving help. What can we do to persist and not lose
faith when answers don't come quickly?

First of all, I earnestly believe in the Lord's great love for his children. As I mention elsewhere in this book, I believe there never was a sincere prayer offered since the days of Adam, by anyone, member or nonmember alike, that was not answered by the Lord. When one truly knows the great love the Lord has for his children, he will know with a certainty that the Lord does answer all sincere prayers.

The key, then, is for us to discern how those answers come. We must not judge the Lord, nor should we harden our hearts when seemingly an answer has not come. Instead, we need to trust the Lord and know he is answering our prayers in his own way and by his own means. As Isaiah taught us:

> For my thoughts are not your thoughts, neither are your ways my ways, saith the Lord.
> For as the heavens are higher than the earth, so are my ways higher than your ways, and my thoughts than your thoughts. (Isaiah 55:8–9.)

I bear my testimony that this is true. Therefore, we cannot judge the Lord—but we can trust him.

Let's look at some of the circumstances where prayers may seem to be unanswered—and how we might understand them.

KNOW THAT ANSWERS MAY COME IN UNEXPECTED WAYS

One kind of seemingly unanswered prayer comes when the Lord does not answer our prayers in the way we expect. If we are more open to the different ways that answers come, we will recognize the Lord's hand in our lives more—and that, in turn, will build our faith so we can receive more answers.

I once had a difficult experience in Guayaquil, Ecuador, that illustrates this. I was on my way to a mission tour in Santa Cruz, Bolivia, with an overnight stop in Guayaquil. The next day, when I arrived at the immigration checkpoint in the Guayaquil airport, I had one hour to go before flight time. As I went through, one of the immigration officers looked at the visa in my passport and said, "You have to obtain proof that you do not have debts in this country. You cannot leave without some financial affidavits. Where are the papers?" I told him that I had never heard of that before, but he said it was necessary and that I could not leave the country.

I explained that I had left the country many times before and that no one had ever asked me for such information in the past. He said it didn't matter and pulled out a long statement of rules proving his assertion that with my kind of visa the financial affidavits were necessary.

Finally the immigration officer next to him got involved. He spoke with him a bit and persuaded him that they should allow me to leave. They stamped my passport and let me go. I was very relieved. I went into the Braniff waiting area and began to read.

After about a half hour, the immigration officer who had allowed me to pass through came up to me and said, "May I see your passport?" I showed it to him, and he took it back to his desk. "I'm sorry," he said, "but I don't think you can leave." He said that allowing me to go would be against the rules and said, "If you did have some kind of debt, we would be responsible for it." Besides, he noted, "You have never been registered into the country."

I continued to talk to him about it, praying silently as I did. Finally he said, "All right, we will let you go this

time, but don't ever come back to Guayaquil unless you
have all your papers in proper order."

I felt very relieved and totally relaxed, convinced
there would be no further problem. I sat and continued
my reading. When they called for the boarding, the few
passengers waiting to board quickly checked through the
door. I began to button up my briefcase to walk through
myself, but the other immigration official came up to me
and said, "Let me see your passport." I asked him what
he needed it for, but he wouldn't tell me. "Let me see it,"
he repeated.

I told him I wouldn't allow him to see it unless he
told me what he wanted. I also said that the other immigration officer had already checked me out of the country and that Braniff had called for boarding. I needed to
board immediately.

He became angry and said, "Follow me," so I walked
back to the immigration desk. He demanded to see my
passport again, telling me that he just wanted to check
something, so I gave it to him. I was becoming increasingly anxious, since all the other passengers had already
boarded. He took my passport and, using his pen, obliterated the stamp his co-worker had put in it. He then
handed the passport back to me and said, "Now let's see
you leave Ecuador. You will not be going today, and you
probably will have to return to Quito to get the paper
you need, and then maybe in a day or so you'll be able to
leave."

I tried to explain that I was the president of an area in
the Mormon Church in those countries and that I had
two hundred missionaries waiting for me. It was all to no
avail; he wouldn't even listen. I didn't know if he was
having a bad day, if he didn't like North Americans, or if

he didn't like Mormons—or all of the above—but he certainly seemed to be determined to cause me difficulties.

When nothing else would work, I demanded to see his boss. He told me he didn't have one and wouldn't give me his name. Finally a lady at a nearby desk said she would give me the number of the immigration department downtown. But she and the man I was dealing with both said I would have to use a public telephone. Unfortunately, I had no coins for a phone. I knew they were stalling me so that I would miss my plane. I informed them I would use their phone and picked it up (to their astonishment) and began to dial. It was only then that I really began to fervently pray in my heart for help. Up until then I had relied on my own strength.

Then I realized it wouldn't help even if I could reach their boss downtown. I would still miss the plane as they sorted things out. I felt inspired to hang up the phone, grab my things, and run out to the Braniff desk. At that moment I saw the more helpful immigration officer walk in off the street. "What are you doing here?" he asked. "I thought you had left." I explained my problem and he looked at my passport, seeing where the other immigration officer had totally obliterated the approval stamp to leave the country.

He walked me back in and asked his co-worker to give him the stamp. The obstinate man refused. The man helping me literally grabbed the stamp from him, restamped my passport so it was legible, and said, "Go!" I did not have to be told twice. I raced onto the Braniff plane just as they were closing the door.

It took me a half hour to regain my composure. I was somewhat in an emotional state after all that difficulty.

After I had calmed down, I gave thanks to the Lord for helping me to finally get onto the plane. It was only then that I remembered a prayer I had offered earlier. About twenty minutes before I had gone through the immigration checkpoint, I had silently prayed that the Lord would help to strengthen my faith. I had asked that he would help me to be willing to pass through any tribulation he might desire, that I would be able to demonstrate my faith under any adversity.

As I contemplated the experience, I was pleased that things had worked out well in the end. But I felt bad that I had not recognized earlier that this was an opportunity to exercise my faith in the Lord. I had asked for an opportunity to grow more, but in the midst of the trial I had forgotten all about it. Instead, I went charging through, relying on my own strength. I was doing more of my part than I needed to, and I didn't let the Lord come in to help when he would have. I was disappointed that I didn't realize until it was all over that that difficult experience had the markings of a blessing—a blessing I had actually asked for, and one I had nearly missed.

BE PREPARED FOR INCREASED OPPOSITION FROM SATAN

If you're praying for something that really matters, you can count on the fact that the devil will get involved. He's eager to do what he can to thwart you. He will do his best to dissuade you from going forward. He'll give you such thoughts as "You can't do it. You're not worthy enough. Your family's got too many problems. You can't do what the Lord requires." He'll engineer whatever he can to try to make you doubt. So you may as well know up front that he is going to tempt you.

When you attract the devil's attention and he starts to give you more opposition than you normally have, that's a great sign that you're on a course that pleases God and displeases Satan.

I've found that when you begin to pray for something that really matters, many times things get worse, not better. Often the cause is Satan and his helpers, who are doing their best to make sure you don't succeed. That ought to be a signal to a man or woman of faith: "I'm on the right track. I'm doing something that's making a difference and I will now double my faith." If you can increase your faith in that moment, you will have won most of the battle.

BE PREPARED FOR THE LORD TO TEST YOUR FAITH

When we're seeking answers to prayers, the Lord will surely test us. He wants us to see if we will serve and love him at any cost. He wants us to see if we will continue in faith even if we don't receive the answer we had hoped for.

The blessing often comes after a trial of our faith (see Ether 12:6), and we have to persevere even through difficult times if we want to come to the answer we seek.

Here is an experience that illustrates that:

I had great desires to be home with my wife at the birth of our sixth child, a son, who was to be delivered in Quito, Ecuador. And she wanted very badly for me to be with her. She didn't speak Spanish very well at that time, and she was uncomfortable with some of the medical procedures there. I arranged my schedule so that I would be home for two or three weeks around the time of the birth of the baby.

Then, to our surprise, the Brethren in Salt Lake City assigned me to go to Brazil for the two weeks immediately prior to the due date. They were unaware of when our baby was due, and we debated whether or not we should tell them. After we carefully considered the options, we determined that we would go forth in faith, hoping that the baby would come at a time when I was present.

The entire family began to pray that the baby would come before I left for Brazil. But it didn't happen, and as I boarded the airplane for Brazil my family all began to pray, "Please do not send the baby now; please wait until Daddy can be home." The Lord blessed us, and the baby did not come while I was in Brazil.

When I got back home to Ecuador, I informed my wife that the Brethren had adjusted the time for the mission president's seminar in Peru; in less than a week I was being asked to go to Peru for four more days.

At that point we were exactly on the expected date of our baby's arrival. That night as my wife and I talked and prayed about the matter, she once again said in great faith, "You go forward and fulfill your assignment. I hope with all my heart that the Lord will allow you to be present for the baby's birth, but if you are not able to be here I will happily do my best to make it on my own. However, I believe that the spirit and authority that calls you to go on these assignments is the same spirit and authority that sends new babies. I can only hope and pray that the Lord will hear us and that you will be present."

I am convinced that at that moment my wife paid the price (the sacrifice) the Lord required for her to receive the blessing—she truly was willing to submit happily to the will of the Lord, whatever it might be.

I went off to Peru for the mission presidents' seminar. On the morning of the fourth day, Elder Howard W. Hunter of the Quorum of the Twelve, who presided at the seminar, told me that I must go home. I said, "Well, the seminar is over tomorrow and then I'll go." He said,

"No, you must go home right now, this very morning." He insisted—and it turned out that his direction was pure inspiration.

I found a flight that morning and left Cuzco, where the seminar was being held, and flew to Lima, then made a connection to fly to Quito, Ecuador. I was met there by one "very pregnant" lady. Upon my arrival at home I rested for a half hour; then my wife said, "It's time. Let's go!" Off we went to the hospital where our sixth child was delivered, a baby boy. I had been home only two hours when he was born.

How kind the Lord was to us in that circumstance. What faith was manifested by my good wife and children, despite the trials and seeming setbacks.

We can truly see that a family united in prayer can have real spiritual power because of their faith. I honestly believe that if a family is praying for what is honorable and right, they have every right to assume that the Lord will respond to them. He will either bless them with what they desire, or give them some indication of why they cannot have it, or indicate that they ought to quit praying for something they will not receive. It was truly satisfying to our family to have our prayers answered in that way.

All the Lord wants from us is to know where our hearts are. If our hearts are right we may receive the trials, but it won't diminish our faith. Or we may not be required even to receive the trials if the Lord feels that we have already gained the benefit that would come from them. Sometimes the Lord will "pull the rug out from under you" in order to be sure of your heart. He may let you pass through difficult circumstances, contrary to what you may have prayed for, just to help you prove to yourself that you really will do anything he might ask you to submit to.

SOMETIMES THE ANSWER COMES LATER

Prayers for the Redemption of Zion. The redemption of Zion gives us a good example of this principle. How many prayers do you think were offered for the redemption of Zion in Missouri in the early part of this dispensation? Once the Latter-day Saints learned they were to build a Zion in Independence, Missouri, don't you suppose that thousands of people would have offered thousands of prayers that they would indeed be able to inherit Zion? Yet, if we judge from the vantage point of those people who were driven out of Missouri, we would have to say that their prayers were not answered.

Yet, because the Lord does things in his own way and in his own time, all of those prayers, in my judgment, have been and will be answered upon the heads of the faithful Latter-day Saints. It is true that they did not appear to be answered then, but that is no reason to assume they are not going to be answered at all. They will be answered, and they will be consecrated for the good of the Saints who offered them.

The Lord said,

> But behold, I say unto you that ye must pray always, and not faint; that ye must not perform any thing unto the Lord save in the first place ye shall pray unto the Father in the name of Christ, that he will consecrate thy performance unto thee, that thy performance may be for the welfare of thy soul. (2 Nephi 32:9.)

These Saints did pray fervently for the redemption of Zion, and, as a result, the Lord will consecrate their performance for the welfare of their souls.

One of the problems we have is that we want our answers and we want them now. Too often we're like the man who prayed for patience and in his prayer added, "And I want it now." Or, to use another example, we may pray for courage and then be astonished when the Lord sends us a lion. We sometimes want the gift without doing the work to obtain it. Facing up to a "lion" will help us to have courage. But if we are not careful, we will not see the lion as a blessing, as an answer to prayer. Instead, we may misjudge the Lord and think we received the opposite. We wanted courage and now we're filled with fear. But the Lord has answered the prayer: He is providing a means for us to participate in the development of that courage and thus participate in the answer to our own prayer.

The Lord answers our prayers in his own way. Some answers come quickly. Some come many, many years later. Some come as we expected. Some come in disguise. But all honest, sincere prayers are answered.

The Prayers of the Nephites. Let me illustrate further with another example. Think of all the prayers that were offered in the times of the Nephites and Lamanites to preserve the Book of Mormon record, as well as the prayers that were offered for the record to come forth. Hundreds of years later these prayers were answered.

> And, behold, all the remainder of this work does contain all those parts of my gospel which my holy prophets, yea, and also my disciples, desired in their prayers should come forth unto this people.
>
> And I said unto them, that it should be granted unto them according to their faith in their prayers;
>
> Yea, and this was their faith—that my gospel, which I gave unto them that they might preach in their days, might come unto their brethren the Lamanites, and also all that had become Lamanites because of their dissensions.

Now, this is not all—their faith in their prayers was
that this gospel should be made known also, if it were
possible that other nations should possess this land;

And thus they did leave a blessing upon this land in
their prayers, that whosoever should believe in this
gospel in this land might have eternal life. (D&C
10:46–50.)

Did not the Lord fulfill his promise and answer their
prayers? Yes, but once again the answer did not come
until hundreds of years had passed.

I say once more, the Lord will answer our prayers in
his own time and in his own way, and his thoughts are
not our thoughts, and his ways are not our ways. Thus,
let us be very careful to never judge the Lord and say,
"He did not answer my prayer."

Prayers to Open the Doors of the Nations. Think of how
many years President Spencer W. Kimball asked the
Latter-day Saints to pray that the doors to the nations
might be opened to the message of the gospel. For years
faithful Latter-day Saints prayed that prayer daily, and
yet the doors did not open. And then all of a sudden,
when it was time (and I repeat, when it was time), the
Lord answered those united prayers, and the doors of the
nations in eastern Europe, the communist world, and
other nations opened, as it were, in a day.

Once again, it occurred according to the Lord's own
timetable. Let us be patient, then, and recognize the
Lord's love for us; and the next time we are faced with
what seems to be an unanswered prayer, let us trust
more, let us have more faith in the Lord, and in time we
will see that the Lord will answer that prayer.

A Mother's Prayer. To put this in a more personal
realm, I have a wonderful friend whose daughter began
to be wayward when she was about fifteen years old.

How this good mother prayed, along with her husband, that this girl would walk the straight and narrow path. However, the girl's agency was in play, and she determined that she wanted to participate in worldly things. And that's exactly what she did.

The mother increased her faith, increased her prayers, increased her fasting, but seemingly to no avail. She felt her prayers were not answered. Her daughter went astray even more and participated in all the worldly things in which a wayward young lady might participate.

Fortunately for this woman, she went on praying. About five years later, this young lady was touched by the Spirit, repented of her sins, fell in love with a young returned missionary, and was ultimately married in the temple.

This entire process took about ten years. Were the mother's prayers answered? Were they consecrated for her good? I bear testimony that they were and that the Lord does answer prayers—but many times not in the way men desire, nor according to the timetable men would choose.

Our own family has seen the truth of this. In at least two instances we have prayed faithfully for something for about ten years. The answers did not come, but we persisted—and finally we are now seeing the fruits of those prayers.

Strengthening Your Children through Family Home Evening. We could find many other examples. For instance, I'm sure you are aware of people who accepted the First Presidency's promise that if they held family home evening faithfully their children would be strengthened. They understood that home evening would more fully facilitate the redemption of their children. Yet in the process, they have lost some of their children. They've prayed and prayed and still the promise has not been realized. Are these Saints looking for answers in the short run only, not recognizing that the Lord's promises apply not only in this life, but in the life to come?

> What I the Lord have spoken, I have spoken, and I excuse not myself; and though the heavens and the earth pass away, my word shall not pass away, but shall all be fulfilled, whether by mine own voice or by the voice of my servants, it is the same. (D&C 1:38.)

The Lord's word will stand. He will answer the prayers of his people. Prophets have borne testimony that if we as parents faithfully do our part, we can more surely bring our children to salvation. If we believe the promises of the Lord or one of his servants, He will answer our prayers in His own time and in His own way.

SOMETIMES THE ANSWER IS UNCLEAR

When I was younger and prayed fervently for answers to prayers, sometimes I didn't feel I received an answer—and then I wondered if the Lord really did love me. I had prayed earnestly and put my trust in the Lord, exercised faith, fasted, and seemingly received no response from the heavens.

I have realized in later years that in many instances the Lord does not give a direct answer to our prayers, since that would destroy our opportunity to exercise faith. Sometimes he knows an unclear answer or a delayed answer is exactly what we need, for a time, so we will learn to exercise greater faith.

But my experience has been that, even if an answer doesn't seem to come, the Lord will still communicate with you. I believe that if you will watch carefully, he will somehow express his love to you, telling you that you are okay in some other way, independent perhaps of that for which you are praying. In this way he will give you comfort and yet not defeat his purpose of causing you to have more faith. Because of his love, he may not respond directly on the issue you're praying about, but some way, somehow, perhaps through some other means or some other issue in your life, he will whisper into your heart the assurance that he does love you, that he is working with you, and that you are okay.

That sweet whispering of assurance will give you confidence that he has heard your prayer, that he knows the situation, and that, if you will be patient, he will handle the whole matter. I have particularly seen this to be the case when, because of my ineptness or inability, I have tied myself or my circumstances up in knots. If I then will be patient and express my love to the Lord, letting him know I trust him even when there seemingly is no answer, he will *gradually* untie all the knots I have so neatly tied up in my life. And, as those knots are untied, he will give me the final peace and assurance that I am okay.

I hope we all see that this is one of the Lord's great approaches for helping us to develop additional faith. The Lord knows us. He can see things clearly, for both the short term and in the long run, and he will do that which will most benefit each of us individually.

Truly the Lord said through his prophets:

He doeth not anything save it be for the benefit of the world. (2 Nephi 26:24.)

And again, I remember that thou hast said that thou hast loved the world, even unto the laying down of thy life for the world. (Ether 12:33.)

Let me give you another illustration from the life of the Prophet Joseph Smith that shows how the Lord might give an answer that doesn't seem clear. At one time Joseph Smith had a great desire to know when Jesus was going to come again. As we read in Doctrine and Covenants 130:14–17:

> I was once praying very earnestly to know the time of the coming of the Son of Man, when I heard a voice repeat the following:
>
> Joseph, my son, if thou livest until thou art eighty-five years old, thou shalt see the face of the Son of Man; therefore let this suffice, and trouble me no more on this matter.
>
> I was left thus, without being able to decide whether this coming referred to the beginning of the millennium or to some previous appearing, or whether I should die and thus see his face.
>
> I believe the coming of the Son of Man will not be any sooner than that time.

It is important to note that Joseph Smith was praying earnestly. He was not just praying; he was praying earnestly. He had prayed many other times and had his prayers answered with direct revelation. It's very likely he assumed this would be another one of those cases.

Instead, the Lord gave him a very brief and somewhat ambiguous answer: "If thou livest until thou art eighty-five years old, thou shalt see the face of the Son of Man; therefore let this suffice, and trouble me no more on this matter."

As Joseph pondered this answer, he was left with three possibilities, as outlined in the following verse: (1) that before Joseph was eighty-five years of age the Lord would come in the Millennium, (2) that the Lord had reference to Joseph Smith seeing his face in a pre-Millennial appearance; or (3) that Joseph might die and thus see his face.

Did Joseph Smith receive an answer to his prayer? One might say with a smile, "Yes, I guess not." He did, but he wasn't absolutely sure what the answer meant. Many times that's the way answers to prayers come to us. Then, as I mentioned before, we have an opportunity to increase our faith even more than if the answer had come clearly.

The key is to not harden your heart, to not be angry with the Lord, and to not, in disbelief, think that he did not answer your prayer. When we have a prayer that doesn't seem to be answered, do we doubt the Lord? Or are we filled with fear, believing we are not adequate or worthy to receive answers to our prayers? We must watch out for such feelings, because they can give Satan an opportunity, through our own doubts and fears, to destroy the faith that we might have otherwise had.

SOMETIMES THE ANSWER WE DESIRE IS NOT GRANTED

Let me share with you a similar story that didn't work out so well. When we were in Uruguay presiding over a mission, we were having another baby. My wife was overdue, and the doctor said that they would induce labor by Monday morning if the labor pains didn't start on their own. We didn't feel like inducing labor was the thing to do—we had a great desire for the baby to come naturally. We decided to ask the missionaries in the office staff to fast and pray with us that the baby would come before Monday.

My wife and I walked more in the next three or four days than we had in the whole month previous, trying to help things along. But the days came and went, and still no baby. On Sunday night we prayed extra fervently, and we continued to pray until 9:30 A.M. on Monday, when the nurse inserted the needle that started the labor.

This experience in prayer seemed to be one of failure, but it really was a success, and it helps to illustrate an important principle of power in prayer.

When our prayers are not answered the way we'd hoped, how do we respond? Do we turn our backs on the Lord in frustration or anger? Do we doubt the process? Do we doubt ourselves? Or do we learn from the experience and continue with increased faith the next time?

I believe that no exercise of faith and prayer is wasted, even if the desired result is not obtained. Every such exercise helps us to grow and develop in most important spiritual ways, and we thereby become more prepared to seek and receive answers to prayers on future occasions.

Of course, all sincere prayers are answered. But remember that sometimes the answer will be no; or yes, but later; or yes, but with alterations; or some other response.

As I conclude this experience, there is one more key observation I feel I should make. Some months later we joined the missionaries in exercising faith, seeking the Lord's blessings in regard to a challenge the mission was having. Suddenly I realized that our earlier efforts to exercise faith (for the natural birth) were now bearing fruit. Because we had tried to *double our faith* when we had "failed" to avoid the inducing of labor, the Lord had truly increased our faith. This earlier, "easy" experience had helped to prepare us to have sufficient faith to face the difficult challenge the mission was now facing.

When you face "failure" in prayer, if you will respond

by praying more, loving the Lord more, trusting more, asking again, and refusing to give up, your faith will be rewarded.

THE LORD WILL DO WHAT IS BEST FOR YOU

It seems many times that the Lord will not reveal his total will to us so that he might give us an opportunity to truly exercise faith. I have a testimony that the Lord will always do that which is good or right for us. I am impressed with these words in Moses 6:32:

> And the Lord said unto Enoch: Go forth and do as I have commanded thee, and no man shall pierce thee. Open thy mouth, and it shall be filled, and I will give thee utterance, for all flesh is in my hands, and I will do as seemeth me good.

It is evident to me that the Lord will treat all men in such a way; he will always do that which is for their best good. We find that same concept taught regarding the families of Joseph Smith and Sidney Rigdon, who had been away from their families for a period of time preaching the gospel. The Lord said to them:

> Verily, thus saith the Lord unto you, my friends Sidney and Joseph, your families are well; they are in mine hands, and I will do with them as seemeth me good; for in me there is all power.
> Therefore, follow me, and listen to the counsel which I shall give unto you. (D&C 100:1–2.)

The Lord often says, "I will do that which seemeth me good." But since we know that he does only that which will benefit mankind, we can also be confident that he will do only that which is best for us. At the same time, it's also clear that he does not reveal to us the totality of his will. He does this so that we can go forward in faith, believing. We are not always certain what he will do or what he will not do, but we know we can trust him to do that which will be the greatest blessing to us.

Questions to Ponder

1. Why do answers sometimes come in ways we do not expect?

_____

_____

_____

2. How will Satan seek to deter us from seeking answers to prayers?

_____

_____

_____

3. Why does the Lord test our faith?

_____

_____

_____

4. When an answer seems to be delayed, how can you persist without giving way to doubt or fear?

_____

_____

_____

5. When answers are unclear, how can you continue to trust in the Lord without becoming frustrated or discouraged?

_____

_____

_____

6. Even when the Lord doesn't give you the answer you expect, what kind of response *will* he give?

_____

_____

_____

7. When things don't work out the way you'd hoped, how can you "double your faith"?

_____

_____

_____

CHAPTER 9

APPLYING THE
PRINCIPLES OF PRAYER

We've talked about some great principles of prayer, but how can we keep track of it all? Over the years I've used a summary of six key points that are easy for me to remember. Then, whenever I'm working on really exercising my faith in prayer, I check my effort against these key principles.

A PROCESS FOR EXERCISING FAITH

Believe. The first thing to remember is the simple word *believe.* By that I mean to have faith, to not doubt, to not have fear. Jesus said you must believe first, then you would see the blessing:

> I say unto you, What things soever ye desire, when ye pray, believe that ye receive them, and ye shall have them. (Mark 11:24.)

When you start praying, you've got to believe as if your request has already been granted. That's the kind of belief the Lord is talking about. Of course, our belief and our faith are in Jesus Christ, who has both the power to grant blessings and the desire to do so. We must always center this belief in Christ, knowing that he will do what

152

is best for us and trusting that our prayers will be answered according to his will.

Repent. The next thing to remember is to repent. Part of repentance is to "sacrifice, to pay the price." We need to find out what we need to change in our lives, what we need to do differently, and then we need to do it.

I'm not surprised that these first two requirements are also the first two principles of the gospel: to have faith in the Lord Jesus Christ and to repent of our sins. After those, we partake of the power and blessing of the ordinances, not just once, but repeatedly. By reliving the ordinances (by partaking of the sacrament and returning to the temple) we can receive strength over and over again as the weeks go by.

Pray. The third key to remember is to pray as if everything depends on God. By trusting in him, by relying on his strength and power, we receive strength and power unto ourselves to see us through to the end.

Work. The fourth principle is to work as if everything depends on us. A great example of this is the story of Nephi, when he went back to Jerusalem to get the brass plates. He and his brothers tried one thing after another as they sought to obtain the plates; and they "failed" each time. But Nephi wouldn't give up. He knew it was the Lord's will that they succeed, and he wasn't going to quit until he had done all in his power to accomplish his purpose. (See 1 Nephi 3–4.)

This story contains another great principle: The Lord reveals his will many times in half steps. He does this so that we will be pressed into exercising faith in order to receive the next step. We might think of this principle as walking to the edge of the light. We must do all in our power, walking to the edge of the light we have and maybe a little way into the dark, and then the lights of revelation will turn on again. But until we walk to the edge of the light and do all in our power to perform, we will often not be ready to receive more from the Lord.

Prepare for intense trials. Number five is to prepare for intense trials of your faith. Remember that when you begin to truly seek answers to prayer, there will be forces that will do all in their power to stop you. So don't be surprised when opposition comes; in fact, you should expect it from the beginning. Then, when difficulties really descend upon you and you reach your bleakest moment, you have the opportunity to discover how much faith you really do have.

Will you stand tall and strong in the face of all adversity? Will you still believe? Will you continue to press forward? Will you pay the price until you've received the blessing from the Lord (or until he tells you it's no longer his will that you seek it)? Do these things and you will endure the trials well, and you'll be that much closer to receiving the blessings you seek.

Expect to see the arm of the Lord revealed. Number six is to expect to see the arm of the Lord revealed on your behalf. Because you've done the things the Lord required, you now have full reason to believe that the Lord will intervene and assist you.

I like the way these ideas encapsulize what is required in receiving answers to prayer. Remember them, ponder them when you're trying to obtain an answer, and evaluate yourself:

Do I really *believe?* Do I have faith in the Lord and his promises?

Am I repentant of my sins?

Do I pray as if all depends on the Lord?

Do I work as if everything depends on me?

Am I prepared to endure intense trials of my faith?

After I've done all these things, do I honestly expect to see the arm of the Lord revealed on my behalf?

When you are in the midst of the battle and need extra assistance, remember the Lord's requirements and his promises, and you'll be able to move ahead more surely.

THE LORD STANDS READY

I bear testimony that the Lord stands ready to answer our prayers and to grant our righteous requests. There is a great example of this in the book of Alma. I've saved this story as a testimony for this last chapter.

Early one morning as our family was reading the account of the wars in Alma, one of my children said, "Dad, I'm not getting much out of these chapters about the wars. I wish we were back reading some of those other things." I answered, "Well, these things are all in here for a good reason, Son. I'm sure there are some hidden treasures in here we just haven't found."

That very morning we found a wonderful description of how the Lord responds to our prayers. In Alma 58 we read how the Lamanites and Nephites were in the midst of a battle. The Nephites were about to lose. They hadn't been too faithful, but when they found themselves in trouble, they went to the Lord for help.

"Therefore," the Nephites said, "we did pour out our souls in prayer to God, that he would strengthen us and deliver us." (Alma 58:10.) What a beautiful description of what we often ask for—to be strengthened or to be delivered from a problem.

Then we get another clue about prayer. The Nephites didn't just pray, but they prayed fervently: "We did pour out our souls in prayer." That's how we get answers—to pray with great intensity.

Now note in this next verse how quietly the answers came. The Lord did indeed answer them, but they might have missed the answer if they weren't being spiritually attentive.

> Yea, and it came to pass that the Lord our God did visit us with *assurances* that he would deliver us; yea, insomuch that he did speak *peace* to our souls, and did grant unto us great *faith,* and did cause us that we should *hope* for our deliverance in him. (Alma 58:11; italics added.)

It may be that the Nephites hoped for a miracle. Maybe they wanted angels to come to deliver them, as had happened a time or two in the Old Testament. But what did they receive? The Lord gave them *assurance, peace, faith,* and *hope.* He didn't directly destroy their enemies, but he did give them the gifts they needed so they could deliver themselves.

The next verse shows the effect of the Lord's answer on the people:

> We did take courage with our small force which we had received [and you may feel that your force or power to accomplish your desires is awfully small], and were fixed with a determination to conquer. (Alma 58:12.)

In other words, the Lord put inside these men the will and the power to do what they desired—to begin with a strong resolve and then to see it through. After their prayer was answered, the Nephites went on to secure their liberty.

When the Lord instills hope and faith and peace and assurance in people, they can bring great things to pass. This, then, is often what we should look for when we ask for help—not a miracle to solve our problem for us, but a miracle inside, to help us come to the solution ourselves, with the Lord's help and the Lord's power.

A WITNESS OF THE TRUTH

As I conclude this book, I would like to bear witness to the truthfulness of that which I've said. I bear witness of a God who loves us. He knows where our hearts are. He lives every moment with each of us. He has borne our pains, afflictions, temptations, sicknesses, and all our infirmities. (See Alma 7:11–12.) He even says that in the last day, when he comes, we will see that "in all [our] afflictions he was afflicted. And the angel of his presence saved [us]; and in his love, and in his pity, he redeemed [us], and bore [us], and carried [us] all the days of old." (D&C 133:53.) I am confident that his angels have saved us numerous times and we knew it not. Can anyone deny his great love for us?

I bear testimony that your faith in the Lord Jesus Christ and your resolve to go forward can combine to bring real power to your life. If you'll nurture and strengthen those feelings, you will have a greater desire to align your will with the will of the Lord—and then you'll soon see your righteous desires become reality.

I hope as you conclude this book that you will seek in prayer to be filled with a fixed determination to conquer . . . to humble yourself more . . . to pray more fervently . . . to believe . . . to repent of your sins . . . to abide the laws and conditions that govern that which you desire. As you do, you'll draw closer to the Lord. And you'll recognize that your prayers are being answered more and more consistently.

Let us therefore never harden our hearts in disbelief and doubt and think that the Lord does not answer prayer. He will never forsake us. Let these great words from the apostle Paul, speaking of the Lord's love, ring in all of our ears:

> Likewise the Spirit also helpeth our infirmities: for we know not what we should pray for as we ought: but the Spirit itself maketh intercession for us with groanings which cannot be uttered.
>
> And he that searcheth the hearts knoweth what is the mind of the Spirit, because he maketh intercession for the saints according to the will of God.
>
> And we know that all things work together for good to them that love God, to them who are the called according to his purpose. . . .
>
> What shall we then say to these things? If God be for us, who can be against us? . . .
>
> Who shall separate us from the love of Christ? shall tribulation, or distress, or persecution, or famine, or nakedness, or peril, or sword? . . .
>
> Nay, in all these things we are more than conquerors through him that loved us.
>
> For I am persuaded, that neither death, nor life, nor angels, nor principalities, nor powers, nor things present, nor things to come,
>
> Nor height, nor depth, nor any other creature, shall be able to separate us from the love of God, which is in Christ Jesus our Lord. (Romans 8:26–28, 31, 35, 37–39.)

These are the sure promises of the Lord. And, concerning his promises, he has said:

> What I the Lord have spoken, I have spoken, and I excuse not myself; and though the heavens and the earth pass away, my word shall not pass away, but shall all be fulfilled, whether by mine own voice or by the voice of my servants, it is the same.
>
> For behold, and lo, the Lord is God, and the Spirit

beareth record, and the record is true, and the truth
abideth forever and ever. Amen. (D&C 1:38–39.)

Questions to Ponder

1. How might the summary of the processes for exercising faith
help you?

_____

_____

_____

2. Why does the Lord often reveal his will in half steps rather
than giving us the whole picture at once?

_____

_____

_____

3. What does the account in Alma teach us about praying with
intensity?

_____

_____

_____

4. We often seek a miracle when instead the Lord desires to
give us peace, assurance, hope, faith, and the will and power
to accomplish that which needs to be done. What in your life
do you need more help with? How can you receive more
peace, assurance, hope, faith, and power to help you in that
thing?

_____

_____

_____

INDEX